LAST MAN STANDING

LAST MAN STANDING

NORMAN COLLINS

The Memoirs, Letters & Photographs of a Teenage Officer

Edited by
RICHARD VAN EMDEN

Pen & Sword
MILITARY

This book is dedicated
to my parents
Wolfgang and Joan van Emden

Other books by the author:

Tickled to Death to Go
The Memoirs of a Cavalryman in the First World War

Veterans
The Last Survivors of the Great War

Prisoners of the Kaiser
The Last POWs of the Great War

The Trench

First published in Great Britain in 2002 by Leo Cooper
Reprinted in 2012 by
PEN & SWORD MILITARY
An imprint of
Pen & Sword Books Ltd
47 Church Street
Barnsley
South Yorkshire
S70 2AS

ISBN 978 1 84884 865 8

Printed and bound in England
By CPI Group (UK) Ltd, Croydon, CR0 4YY

Pen & Sword Books Ltd incorporates the Imprints of Pen & Sword Aviation,
Pen & Sword Family History, Pen & Sword Maritime, Pen & Sword Military,
Pen & Sword Discovery, Wharncliffe Local History, Wharncliffe True Crime,
Wharncliffe Transport, Pen & Sword Select, Pen & Sword Military Classics,
Leo Cooper, The Praetorian Press, Remember When,
Seaforth Publishing and Frontline Publishing

For a complete list of Pen & Sword titles please contact
PEN & SWORD BOOKS LIMITED
47 Church Street, Barnsley, South Yorkshire, S70 2AS, England
E-mail: enquiries@pen-and-sword.co.uk
Website: www.pen-and-sword.co.uk

CONTENTS

Acknowledgements

My especial thanks must go, first and foremost, to Norman's son, Ian Collins, whose patience, encouragement and kindness have been unfailing. I am very grateful to Ian for entrusting to me all of Norman's possessions from his service in the Great War, including all his notebooks and photographs.

I should also like to thank the staff of the Department of Documents in the Reading Room of the Imperial War Museum. As keepers of Norman's letters and postcards - sent during his service at home and at the front - they have all been extremely helpful during my frequent visits to the archive.

Many thanks must go to Roni Wilkinson at Pen and Sword Books who, as usual, has put up with the shenanigans of Richard van 'Whatsit', as I have always affectionately been known to him. Roni has produced a book that Norman would have been proud of, as I am. I must also thank both Charles Hewitt and Brigadier Henry Wilson at Pen and Sword Books for their continued faith in me.

A very big extra thank you must go to my parents, Joan and Wolfgang van Emden. My books are invariably dumped on them at short notice as deadlines draw near, yet they never fail to cast their eyes over a text where, inevitably, there are important corrections to be made. Their efficient editing of this book has been invaluable, as has my father's translation of a letter written in German and found by Norman in 1917, (see page 151)

I would also like to thank Anna, my partner, whose encouragement and cups of coffee have been unending, despite her own high-pressure job.

Finally, there are many others whom I would like to thank for various and disparate reasons, including Steve Humphries, Peter Barton, Dave Bilton, Steve Grogan and Vic and Diane Piuk.

Introduction

It has been commonly said that the average 'life' expectancy at the front of a Second Lieutenant in World War One was approximately six weeks before he was either killed or wounded. In this respect, and in this one respect only, my friend Norman Collins was no better than average. He arrived on the Somme in late October 1916 and was wounded in early December – six weeks. In late April 1917 he returned to France and was slightly wounded in late May – five weeks; then he was wounded for the third and final time in the second week of July – six weeks. His 17 weeks at the front were to put him in hospital for a total of 14 months and give him a lifetime of pain that no disability pension could ever compensate for.

I knew Norman for only three years but in that limited time I found him in every other way exceptional. I met him through my work in television, when a colleague happened to mention that Norman had contacted the company in response to an appeal for veterans of the First World War. Norman, as I was to find out, had already been seen on television, in BBC2's Nineties series; he had also appeared in a couple of Imperial War Museum books.

We quickly found that Norman was one of those rare veterans who had an almost photographic recall of his war service and it was decided that we should film him straight away. In the end, we recorded his memories for at least three different programmes, such was his clarity of mind and eloquence of speech.

With most interviewees, contact is sadly fleeting and usually finishes after the broadcast of the programme, but I found Norman so fascinating that I returned to see him, and a friendship developed. In time, I was very proud to be invited to his 100th birthday in 1997, and very sad, yet honoured, to attend his funeral in February 1998. Even now, it doesn't seem possible that Norman has been dead for

Norman Collins aged one hundred.

Norman (top) *aged 18 months and* (bottom) *on his seventh birthday. He is pictured with his elder brother Bolton.*

over four years. He was one of those people who will always stay alive to those who met him and therefore will never quite seem gone. This book is, I hope, a fitting tribute to him.

When I met Norman, he had recently moved to a village close to Peterborough, a town which had been his home for many years, and where he lived in what was reputedly the town's oldest house. As Norman's eyesight had deteriorated, he had moved in with his son, Ian, cementing yet further a very close relationship between the two. Even though Ian's work frequently took him overseas, they spoke daily on the phone. As Norman became less mobile and his war injuries caused him considerable pain, he took to tape recording a daily diary of the events around him as well as his own recollections of his long life. Invariably his war memories came to the fore and tapes sometimes labelled just "Random Recollections" often held invaluable details from his war story. These tapes could have become the basis of a biography and indeed, during one of my visits, Norman mentioned that he was looking for someone to write his story. Although inwardly enthusiastic to volunteer, I felt unable to offer through pressure of work. Nevertheless, I had a recurrent and niggling feeling that I was passing up a wonderful opportunity. From that moment onwards, I felt certain that I would return to Norman's story.

It was not just the clarity of Norman's recall that made the prospect of a book so exciting. Many memoirs written by veterans have been remarkable for their detail, as have those ghost-written in recent years by friends and enthusiasts. Norman won no awards for gallantry; he wasn't even at the front for very long, and while he was there he was, for the most part, the most junior of junior officers. However, unlike almost every memoir in print, Norman's had something else to offer. He had every postcard he sent during his war service, and albums of photographs shot from 1917 onwards on a little Vest Pocket Kodak (VPK) camera bought while on convalescence. This remarkable collection of items was supplemented by other rarities and included both notebooks written during training and memorabilia picked up from the battlefields of France and Belgium. Lastly, there was a series of pictures taken of Norman when he returned to the Western Front for the one and only time when aged 92 in 1989. With taped interviews that I had conducted with Norman in his later years, this was a collection of material unlikely to be replicated.

The letters in particular are fascinating. Their survival was thanks not to Norman but to his brother, Bolton. Norman had no knowledge of the letters' existence until his brother died in 1971. Bolton had kept every scrawled note from the first day of Norman's army service, every letter written from the trenches and later from hospital. With Bolton's death, his widow felt it appropriate that they be given back to their author, much to Norman's great surprise and delight.

The letters are all the more interesting because they were never written for public consumption. Norman posted

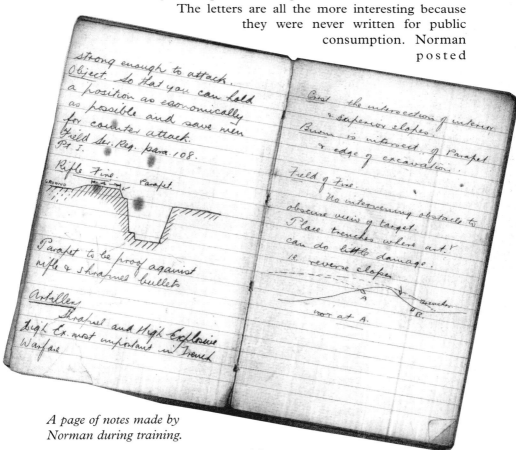

A page of notes made by Norman during training.

11

his letters home in the belief that they would probably end up in the family waste bin or fire. They were therefore written without any thought to their later historical significance or appeal. They contain the 'real' unvarnished thoughts of a young World War One private who advanced through every non-commissioned rank before he became a young subaltern, rising to the rank of captain shortly after the war's end. In all there were 170 letters and 42 postcards sent at regular intervals from wherever Norman happened to be.

The photographs Norman took are equally interesting, as few pictures of life in France were taken by British soldiers because such images contravened Army regulations. However, while any soldier caught with a camera might face court martial, many middle ranking officers appear to have happily turned a blind eye to the amateur photographers. Even though few pictures were taken in the front line, most show life close to the front. There are powerful images of officers and men, many of whom would not survive the war. Unfortunately most pictures are not annotated and one can't help looking at the faces of officers and other ranks, and wondering 'Did you survive?'

There are some notable images. There is a picture of James Pollock, who won the Victoria Cross. There is a photo of B.L Jacut, a former Royal Flying Corps pilot, who later won bronze in the Olympic 100 metres final behind Johnny Weismuller, aka Tarzan. More poignantly, there is a picture of Private Alexander Simpson, Norman's 18-year old batman, who was to die during the Third Battle of Ypres. His face is clearly that of a boy in 1917; just what did he look like when he went to France for the first time in December 1915, or indeed when he had stood in front of the recruitment sergeant six months to a year earlier?

There is no doubt that Norman was haunted by the memories of his war, although his strength of character and determination to succeed helped him cope with what he had seen. He never forgot those who had died, and in later life his memory of them grew more poignant as he became the last survivor who could recall these men in their youth. The frequency of their deaths at the front greatly troubled Norman during the war and his letters home are littered with references to their early deaths. 'Pitcairn's brother was killed going back to his transport column'. 'You would see the report of Robson's death'. 'Thirty of my Lichfield pals are dead that I know of.' 'My servant went west last week. He was just 19 and had been out two years'. 'Of all the officers who were out with me last year there is only one left in France.'

After 18 months' training, Norman undoubtedly wanted to go to France. He certainly had feelings of trepidation but equally he was excited by the prospect of war. Some of the most interesting letters, indeed some of the most descriptive, stem from his earliest days in

France when, almost with a child's eyes, he soaks up every detail of his surroundings, watching and making mental notes. Despite the tiredness and cold he clearly enjoys the life; he counts barrage balloons and records the numbers of tanks. Even after his first taste of battle he is a keen souvenir collector, and, while claiming to be too busy to collect much, still mentions picking up a German helmet, a pistol, some shoulder straps, a couple of bells, a bayonet and other bits and pieces. Other details stand out, too. His expectation of a ten day leave over Christmas 1916, after just two months in France, is interesting to those who know how much leave other ranks could expect: none for at least six months, while one private known to the author had just two spells of leave, totalling ten days, in four years of fighting.

In later years, as the number of veterans dwindled, Norman became acutely aware of his generation's passing. His affinity with the soldiers of that war reasserted itself and, despite being in his mid-nineties, he sought out local veterans and visited them himself. A small collection of tapes exists on which are recorded his visits to veterans such as ex-artilleryman Norman Tennant, former Seaforth Highlander John Willens, and 104-year-old Ross Morris, ex-6th Northants Regiment. Norman was to outlive all these men; indeed it was one of Norman's last ambitions to be the final survivor of the war. He was certainly one of the very last officers and was believed to be the penultimate surviving Seaforth Highlander. He died on February 2nd 1998, ten days after his wife Helen to whom he had been married for 58 years.

In producing this book, I have acted merely as an editor to Norman's own words written during the war or recorded in recent years. Naturally, not all the letters home are of special interest to the reader and I have edited many to the extent that I have omitted everyday references and pleasantries concerning people at home of

Norman as a newly commissioned officer in 1916.

whom neither the reader nor the editor have any knowledge. I have also sought to edit out any repetition of events in letters to his family, as well as occasional perfunctory and routine references to the weather. To this end, too, I have written out every new address as it appears at the top of each letter but have subsequently omitted it until Norman is seen to move elsewhere. Lastly, Norman wrote many letters with one sentence per paragraph. These have been kept where their use expresses the breathlessness of the events around him. However, given the limited space in this book, I have linked paragraphs where it seemed appropriate or expedient to do so.

Emotionally, Norman never left the battlefields of France and Flanders. His empathy for the men he served with or whom he commanded was very evident to all who met him. When a camera crew followed Norman back to France in 1989 he visited the cemetery of Maillet Wood, where so many of his battalion were buried. After visiting the graves of those he knew, Norman walked slowly to the gate. He turned around, stood for a few seconds and then briefly waved before walking away. The wave spoke volumes.

Richard van Emden
JUNE 2002

CHAPTER ONE

The Enemy at the Gate

On the morning of December 16th 1914 I was sitting having my breakfast porridge. I was seventeen years old and had been working for a year at a local marine engineering company in Hartlepool where I was serving an apprenticeship. I was due to leave for work when, at about 8.10am, a terrific explosion rocked the house. We had two shore batteries sited nearby and during normal firing practice we received prior warning to open our windows to avoid the glass being shattered by the guns' blast, but this was no normal firing practice, for following the inferno of noise there came a reek of high explosive. I didn't know what had happened so I rushed outside. Clouds of brick dust and smoke eddied around me before I ran towards the promenade which was only 50 yards away. On the seafront, half left, were three huge grey German battlecruisers, blazing away, and in the dull light of a winter's morning it was like looking into a furnace. At first I didn't understand the screeching noise that passed over my head like huge pencils on slate, and then I realised they were shells. The ships were firing at the shore batteries of which we had two, each with small six-inch guns. I was fifty yards from the lighthouse battery on what was known as the Heugh Headland. This battery had three naval guns and I could see that they were hammering

German depiction of her battlecruisers closing in on the English east coast, 16 December 1914. Inset: in command of the force and aboard his flagship HIMS Seydlitz, Admiral Franz von Hipper (1863-1932).

away at one ship in particular, although I could not hear them above the blast of the German guns as they belched clouds of flame and smoke.

Each ship had about eight large guns, so that there were about 24 large shells being fired on the town at any one time. I stood there watching them, and, you know, it was an amazing sight to watch broadsides from battlecruisers as close as that.

There would be a broadside, then they turned about and fired another broadside, and this went on for at least half an hour. I was standing at the base of the breakwater where it joined the promenade and I wondered if the Germans were going to land, so I turned away and retraced my steps to my home in Rowell Street and turned left towards the Baptist chapel. A great hole appeared in its stone façade as I approached it.

Walking towards town was one of the silliest things I have ever done, as I was walking into a battlefield, walking among the shells that were exploding. Yet I had no feeling of panic whatsoever. Just as I turned the corner into Lumley Street, I saw the body of Sammy Woods, aged nineteen, a school and Sunday School friend of mine; he was lying half in and half out of his doorway, dead of course. He had been caught by a shell that had fallen to my left into the rectory that belonged to St Hilda's

Images of severe damage after the bombardment. Several affected streets have since been demolished.

Church. A shell had burst just as he stepped out and a second before I turned the corner.

I continued walking. I looked at St Hilda's church. Shells were dropping fairly close but I didn't see any hit, so I kept on going. I walked down towards the docks and I saw the town gasometer receive a hit and of course, with the gas escaping, it went down and collapsed. The shells were dropping too along the dockside, amongst the pit props on the quayside. Now a pit prop is like a tree trunk and was used in the galleries of coalmines, and as this was County Durham we needed thousands of them. As the shells were dropping in amongst them the props were all going up in the air just like boxes of matches, only of course these pit props weighed over a hundredweight each.

I'd never been under fire before and I didn't quite know how it operated. I was just walking through an incident, like a spectator to an event, a heavier bombardment than was probably taking place on the Western Front at that time. I can't remember being frightened. I wouldn't have been human if I wasn't but the whole thing was too much of a shock really, so out of the ordinary, and that suppresses fear.

Having exhausted the view, I walked on into the town, past a wall and under the railway bridge, round to the other side of the docks to where

RY ST. HARTLEPOOL.
ER BOMBARDMENT. DEC. 1914.

*Top right, the rectory, bottom
right 7 Victoria Place where
forty-nine year old William
Avery, an adjutant in the
Salvation Army, was killed.
The insets show the houses as
they appear today.*

BACK OF POST OFFICE. CLEVELAND RD. HARTLEPOOL.

Sir William Grey and Company had their marine works. I wondered what was going on there because nobody had turned up for duty or, if they had, they'd gone. I was looking at the docks from the opposite side but there was nothing new, so I decided then I'd better go back and see what had happened to my parents. I don't know why I hadn't thought of that before. As I made my way back I saw plenty of women running around, screaming, with babies in their arms, trying to get rid of them, to give them to somebody who could help, but there was nobody. I saw two women rush up to a soldier who was obviously trying to make his way to the Garrison, and try and push a baby into his arms. Of course he couldn't do it, he was on duty in any case, so he refused. Then one of the woman came to me, but I also refused. Other people were carrying their most precious possessions. One realist had a mattress on his head as he staggered up Hart Lane.

The noise of the shells began to lessen about 8.50 and finally only the occasional explosion occurred and then silence. A proclamation was made by the mayor and delivered through the town crier. He appeared and started shouting for everyone to keep calm, letting people know that the shelling had stopped and that there was no immediate danger, and no landing had taken place. He informed us that the situation was now secure, whatever that meant! I got back to the promenade and asked someone if they had seen my father. They replied that he had last been seen pushing a wheelchair towards the open country with an invalid in it.

Back home, I found mother in the kitchen making cups of tea for

A collection of German shells that failed to explode.

anyone who wanted one. I thought, 'Well, that's just like mother'. I went in and there she was, as calm as could be, so I began calling on relatives near at hand, and apart from a connection by marriage who had lost a limb in Victoria Place, we had suffered no serious injuries. Later that morning I went and collected pieces of shell. There was debris everywhere. Shell fragments, some weighing several pounds, were being collected as souvenirs and I still have several which came through the roof of our house. They bristle with jagged edges and the mortar is still lodged in the steel. Elsewhere I found a dead donkey that had been grazing in the friarage field, the home ground of the Hartlepool Rovers Rugby Football Club, and I have the piece of shell that killed it.

There was some panic, but not a great deal, as I remember. A lot of people had been killed and wounded and people were being removed from buildings which had been damaged, and taken to hospital. (9 soldiers were killed, 37 children and 97 men and women. 466 were wounded.) I understand that around 1500 shells were fired but they didn't do the damage they were designed to do. A twelve-inch armour piercing shell was intended to be fired against the sides of a battleship that has perhaps twelve inches of armour plating. But in Hartlepool there was nothing to stop the shells going straight through a house, and many failed to explode.

It wasn't all one way. The shore battery I had seen pounding away had scored a direct hit on a gun crew of the *Blücher*. I later found out that the other ships in the raid had been Germany's very latest, the *Moltke* and the *Seydlitz*.

The bombardment of Hartlepool was hushed up to a certain extent because the press said it was an undefended town. This wasn't true as Hartlepool put up a good defence with what it had, indeed the first soldier to be killed on British soil in the Great War died with the Heugh Battery and there is a plaque commemorating the event to this day. The Germans had every right to bombard Hartlepool. Whitby and Scarborough on the other hand were undefended. Although only a few dozen shells were fired into these towns, they took the full publicity for this very reason. Later, when I joined the army at Dingwall, I took some of the photographs of the bombardment taken by a local man, and most of the recruits had never heard of the attack.

A fragment of shell casing picked up by Norman. This piece killed a donkey in the field next to the Friary.

A plaque commemorating those who were killed. The name of Norman's friend Sammy Woods, who was killed as he left his house, can be seen.

BOMBARDMENT.

THE FOLLOWING WERE KILLED IN THE BOMBARDMENT OF HARTLEPOOL DEC. 16TH 1914.

ALLEN.ANNIE
AMBROSE.ROBT L.
ASHCROFT.EDWARD
ASQUITH.WILLIAM
AVERY.WILLIAM G.
BACKHAM.CUTHBT J.
BUNTER.JAMES
CAPELING.N.
CHAPPLE.WM
CLARK.JOHN
COOK.JAMES
CORNER.ANNIE
CORNFORTH. CHAS.
CORNFORTH.JANE A.
CORNFORTH.POLLY
COX.THOMAS G.
CRAKE.JOHN.W.
DIXON.ALBERT
DIXON.GEORGE B.
DIXON.MARGARET E.
GEIPEL.ETHEL M.
HAMILTON.JESSIE
HARPER.ELIZABETH A.
HARRIS.ETTA
HEALEY.JOHN
HERBERT.SELINA
HIGHAM.THOMAS
HODGSON.JOHN
HORSLEY.HILDA
HUDSON.CHAS.W.
JEFFREY.THOMAS
KAY.ANNIE M.
KAY.FLORENCE J.
LEE.CLEMENTINA
LEIGHTON.JOHN S.
MARSHALL.CATH.
MEASOR.CHRIS.
REDSHAW.MARGT A.

STAUNCH.JOHN
STEWART.STANLEY
STRINGER.ETHEL
SWALES.MATTHEW H.
UNTHANK.FRANK
WAINWRIGHT.FREDA
WATSON.MARY B.
WATT.AMY
WHITECROSS.JOHN M.
WHITECROSS.PETER
WILLIAMS.IVY
WOODS.SAMUEL N.
WRIGHT.WILLIAM
YOUNG.BERTIE

CHAPTER TWO

An Edwardian Childhood

I was the second son of Frederick and Margaret Collins and was christened William Norman, although all my life I preferred my second name. My parents and grandparents were good Methodists, clean living, teetotal, and well read. My father, Frederick Collins, worked at the same engineering firm to which I was later to be apprenticed, but his real calling in life was as a lay preacher for over 50 years. His parents had died before I was born but my mother's parents were both still alive during my childhood: my grandmother Margaret Vint (1836-1911) died a week after her 75th birthday, while my grandfather Thomas Bolton (1835-1914) was spared the bombardment of the town by a little less than a month.

I used to have long conversations with my grandfather, as he lived with us at Rowell Street until he died. He was born in Gateshead and told stories of George Stevenson, inventor of the Rocket. I expect it was his father who had known Stevenson, as my grandfather would probably have been too young to work with the great man. He and my grandmother had had eleven children, seven of whom had survived childhood. My father too had been one of eleven children, so I must have had many more cousins than I was ever able to meet.

Norman's grandparents stand at the gate of their house at 12 Beconsfield Square.

23

My mother was the one who looked after the finances. She was very frugal and was able to put down a deposit and take out a mortgage to buy her own house, the family home in Rowell Street, close to where my grandparents owned their home and where I was, in fact, born on April 16th 1897: 12 Beaconsfield Square. This secluded square is off-set from Beaconsfield Street, at the end of which was a small town moor, in reality a headland, as it was only two hundred yards from the lighthouse and the North Sea. The town occupied the whole of a small peninsula that pointed almost directly to Jutland and Germany. On the north side of the town there was a promenade many miles long and a concrete breakwater stretching out for about 500 yards almost due east and dividing the north and south sands. The north sands and seaweed-covered rocks ran for many miles to the left of the breakwater, while to the right Hartlepool Bay lay sheltered to the south west, close by the docks and harbour where ships were built and repaired, or cargoes loaded and unloaded.

The rhythm of the sea, ebbing and flowing, dominated our whole lives and was a constant background, which we did not notice unless the gales of autumn and winter lashed the seas into a frenzy. The waves then pounded the concrete promenade and swept like Niagara Falls over the breakwater which shook and was a spectacular sight. From the north of the promenade there was nothing until the farthest wastes of Spitzbergen and when the northeast wind blew it penetrated anything we wore. It was said that if anyone could survive in old Hartlepool they could survive anywhere in the world.

The chief occupations of the town were shipbuilding, the building of marine engines, and fishing from the shore. All our family, in fact all the families in Hartlepool, either worked on ships or marine engines or they were marine surveyors. Everything was connected with the sea. And those who didn't work there provided the ships' captains, ships' officers and ships' engineers. As children we argued incessantly about the merits of different ships. The *Mauritania* and the *Titanic* were to become part of my boyhood as we discussed every detail of them, even in school. There was great rivalry between the Cunard and the White Star Line at the time and we boys took sides on this too, the *Mauritania* always being my favourite.

South of the breakwater we had a magnificent fish quay and as many as forty steam trawlers lined up to unload their fish. The bustle and stir can only be imagined as the fish, cod, herring, eels, turbot, mackerel, and skate were laid out on the quay, packed into boxes and despatched by rail to various destinations, while there was quite an industry smoking kippers.

It would appear that I was quite a loner as a small boy, and I often wandered around the docks on my own just observing the life around me. Sailing ships were quite common and their bowspits jutted over the edge of the quay and one could walk underneath and look at the figureheads that were made of wood and highly painted. One large ship had the huge head and torso of Neptune and in his hands he grasped this trident, gazing at me with his fierce eyes. As I walked I would see the dark skinned Lascars looking over the rails and I fancied that one day I would

The Elephant Rock at Hartlepool.

sail to the southern seas and see where these men and their ships traded.

On the seaward side of the sands, there was a ledge of rocks leading into the deep water and it was on this coast that so many fine ships were lost. At one time the rocks near Hartlepool must have been quite high, and the last one, about the height of a small church, called the Elephant Rock, was photographed in the year of my birth. It was called the Elephant Rock because of its shape, and must have been a great landmark. It was with a sense of loss that the inhabitants of Hartlepool saw this great edifice finally washed away by the waves, and nothing remains of it in my memory.

I remember two great steamers being wrecked on the rocks. One carried pit props from Scandinavia and the other butter from Denmark. The pit props were stacked high on the decks and were washed over in large rafts of timber. When the waves engulfed the ship, the local inhabitants rushed down to collect them for firewood. Most were recovered by the police, as flotsam belongs to the insurance company – very different from jetsam, which is public property. The other ship carried butter tubs which were seen to bob about on the waves or become lodged among the rocks. These tubs were raided by the inhabitants and again, while these were largely recovered, I'm sure many a pound of Danish butter found its way onto the breakfast table of the people of Hartlepool.

I don't think any lives were lost when these ships foundered but it was a thrilling sight to see the men being rescued by a breeches buoy. First of all a light line was fired towards the ship and this was attached to a heavier cable and drawn across and secured at each end. We rushed down to watch the rescue as soon as we heard the commotion. The breeches buoy slid along a cable attached to the ship and carried two or three of the crew at a time. A searchlight played upon the scene making it all the more exciting as the waves were quite high and sometimes the breeches buoy dipped into the water. The great steam hulks lay for years on the rocks, rusting away.

On this, the north side of the breakwater, the rocks reached right up to the promenade and were covered with seaweed which, when covered by the tide, housed many different kinds of fish. At low tide we used to explore this area and we often used to go out and catch crabs with an iron hook.

The promenade stretched for at least a mile in the direction of Sunderland, and when the sea was bad the waves swept over the promenade and one couldn't walk along there. There was an escape ladder connected to the concrete face of the promenade for anyone who was caught out by the tide. I had to make use of this on one occasion when I was very small. I could hardly reach from one rung of the ladder to the next and when I got to the top of the wall I was unable to reach the railings to pull myself to safety. I had to wait there until I heard footsteps approaching and then saw a pair of legs and shouted with all my might. The man at first couldn't locate the voice but then he saw the top of my head and reached down and pulled me up, asking my name

The house, middle right, at Monk Heseldon where Norman spent much of his childhood. Sadly, the houses were demolished in the early 1960s for a redevelopment that never materialized (see inset).

Norman outside the house at Monk Heseldon with members of his family.

and sending me on my way. I was more than a little shaken and I dreamt about it for years. It was the horror of waiting, clinging on these steps, forty feet above the waves which were coming to catch me up and sweep me away.

We were always warned not to bathe from the north sands, particularly on an ebbing tide, as there was a tremendous undertow and, even when paddling, one had to lean against it as the tide swept out. However, on the calmer side of the breakwater I used to swim in the sea and from the bedroom window my mother could watch my black head in the waves slowly making its way towards the end of the breakwater to the steps, about a quarter of a mile from the shore.

Not far away from here was a part of the town known as The Croft, where the fishermen lived. They were a tough breed and did not mix with the other folk in the town. This was almost a no-go area as it was inhabited by an entirely different race of people from the rest of the town. They had strange names and I think must have been originally French Huguenots. There is an old story that the men of Hartlepool tried and executed a monkey in this part of the town, and it is quite true. During the Napoleonic wars, a monkey was washed ashore from a ship in a storm and was taken for a French spy. Behind The Croft there was the High Street and at the foot of the street there was a large pump and it was from here that the monkey was hung. This was and remains a well known

The pomp of Empire Day at Hartlepool.

story, and on least one occasion during the Great War I was asked, by a fellow officer, 'Who hung the monkey?'

Some of my best memories of childhood took place at a family-owned house in the countryside. In 1887 my grandfather acquired a small cottage in a village called Monk Hesleden, about seven miles north of Hartlepool. I was taken there when I was a few weeks old and, ever since, Monk Hesleden has held a very special place in my affections.

We often holidayed here. The picnic was a highlight because we had all the family with us. They tended to stay on shore and it was rare for anyone to accompany me on my swimming from the rock sands, as father never swam, and mother and my elder brother Bolton couldn't, although I enjoyed watching them paddle. Father was fond of the Dene but never ventured far into the woods. He usually found a comfortable spot in the shade where he could lie down, put a handkerchief over his face to fend off the midges, and had a little snooze. No doubt on these occasions he composed his sermons, which were very popular in the mining district where he served as a lay preacher in the United Methodist Church. His preaching, I was told, was very powerful.

Like many boys of the time, I made bows and arrows and catapults, and tried to knock off a few rabbits, quite successfully on occasions. For catapults we used steel ball bearings that would kill a rabbit easily. The farmers used them in the cornfields as the rabbits converged on the centre when the corn was cut. The arrows were really deadly things. We used to get horseshoe nails and put them on the railway track for the train to run over them. Turned into spearheads with the thick end hammered out like a half crown, the metal would be heated and wrapped round the end of an arrow and then feathered at the other end. I remember once firing one arrow straight up in the air and it went up and up and up before turning over to come down. At that moment two old ladies were walking up the path from the church and I could see that the arrow and the old ladies would shortly converge. The arrow buried itself in the ground right in front of them and they stopped and wondered where it had come from. It was a very near escape, but I really had little sense of danger.

A friend of mine, Fred Chiverton, bought a .22 rifle and we used to line up tins, about four feet from the ground, and fire at them with no background whatever. Later, Fred bought a .410 shotgun which I used

Norman, holding the ball, surrounded by the rest of the Saracens rugby team.

Kruger, the despised Boer leader.

to shoot my first running rabbit. I completely blew away its insides and I was rather shocked by the sight. I then sent away to Gammages and bought a 9mm long barrelled pistol, which was quite legal in those days, and with it I could knock over small birds.

My interest in things military began in earliest childhood. I used to dress up in soldier's clothes, like a toy soldier, belts and things like that, just a bit of fun, but nothing indicative, I think, to show that I was going to be an infantry officer in the Great War. However, the Army held an attraction for me. I remember the Relief of Ladysmith and Mafeking. I must have been about three at the time and I can remember an effigy of Kruger, the Boer President, with his top hat and tails. He was thrown on a large bonfire, the flames of which roared up the figure of this old gentleman amid the loud cheers of the assembled company. The men of the village had a torchlight procession and marched for miles, all around the houses, over the railway bridge, you could see the lights, the flames. There were fireworks too. I held a sort of sparkler and then the big bonfire was lit. I was horrified as a little child – watching the flames, and then poor old Kruger, his hat fell off and he tipped forward and fell into the flames, and I thought it was not a good thing to do to the old man. At the time a new verb entered the English language: it was to 'Maffick', and it meant riotous behaviour while rejoicing or celebrating some momentous event.

I remember the names of the Generals: we had Lord Roberts, General Gordon of Khartoum, and Kitchener too, of course, and even Winston Churchill; he was a war correspondent and was captured by the Boers. We had a great standing then, across the globe, and father told us many, many stories of the British Empire in its heyday. We had a Land of Hope and Glory, the great Cape to Cairo railway, while a third of the world was painted red, marking the extent of the British Empire. And I remember, too, the stories of the war that was to come.

There was a strong cadet force in all public schools and there was a very similar, if milder, corps in the day schools where I went. We weren't issued with rifles but we were taught to drill. I learnt to drill quite well. I could take a squad of boys and number them off and get them into ranks of four and right wheel, left wheel and that sort of nonsense, and this stood me in good stead when I joined the army.

We knew there was going to be a showdown with Germany because they were always drinking a toast to 'Der Tag'. I had an uncle who worked for an engineering company and when he went to Germany he told me all the news about how this war was going to begin. Of course we thought we would take part in it, no doubt. 'Der Tag' – The Day – the day when the war would break out.

Of course we had no conception of what it would be like. Nevertheless, we looked forward to it, and even then we talked about what we were going to do and the regiments we were going to join. I wanted to join a Scottish Regiment because, on my father's side, his grandmother was a Hay and another one a Henderson, so I thought I had enough Scottish blood in me to justify my ambition.

There was no question of feeling frightened about the prospect of war and I think that was partly to do with the literature we were bought. During my boyhood I read as much as I could about the world. I remember reading three books called *Britain Invaded*, *Britain at Bay* and *Britain's Revenge,* which I bound together. I think it was published by the *Boy's Own Paper,* of which I was a great fan, and we knew, of course, that we would win in the end because the book said so.

On the seas, it was laid down that the British navy had to be twice the size of the next largest. As schoolboys in a shipbuilding town, we devoured the statistics of the latest British dreadnoughts, part of the Great British fleet which had 600 vessels by 1914, ready to face anything. Battleship after battleship was completed, the *Iron Duke* was the flagship. Following the great battleships came the battlecruisers and they really captured the imagination. They were very graceful, fast, heavily armed but lightly armoured. There was the *Lion*, which was Admiral Beatty's flagship, the *Tiger*, the *Inflexible*, the *Indomitable*, the *Prince of Wales*, the *Queen Elizabeth*, and many others. The Germans, of course, copied us, so far as they could, and they also built a splendid line of battlecrusiers, including the *Sedlitz*, the *Moltke* and the *von der Tann*.

In 1911 I recall the Army coming to camp at Hesleden. This was really very thrilling to watch. Large numbers of soldiers gathered at High Hesleden in a field in front of the Ship Inn, where there were pitched hundreds of bell tents. Bugles were blowing, bands were practising, the horse lines were formed with the most magnificent officers' chargers. Chestnuts, bays, greys, the harnesses of which glistened with polishing by grooms who seemed to be at it all the time polishing the reins, the horses' bits and chains. That wonderful summer of 1911! We often visited the horse lines, and it was lovely to see these beautiful chargers with their hooves black-leaded and their officers in their smart uniforms. One day they marched from High Hesleden over the bridge into Monk Hesleden, and for the first time I saw an army unit at close quarters. The officers were mounted on their chargers and a Sergeant Major, a fierce looking man, was in charge of the proceedings as far as I could see. I learnt that a battalion of 1,000 men consisted of four companies, A, B, C, D, and each company consisted of four platoons, 1, 2, 3, 4. Each company was commanded by a Major or Captain, each platoon by a Lieutenant,

P32&33 Halcyon days: pre-war soldiers enjoy summer manoeuvres.

Second Lieutenant and a Platoon Sergeant. Each platoon was divided into four sections, each commanded by a Corporal or Lance Corporal. In those days the men marched in column of fours and I saw that many of the men wore the Ribbons of the South African War.

The sound of the bugles was thrilling, especially the sunset ceremony, when the colours were hauled down for the night. These bronzed infantry soldiers marched through the village with packs and rifles on long route marches. They went down into the Dene and up the other side of the valley to Nesbit Hall and disappeared into the distance while we awaited their return. When they came back their shirts were open to the neck and they looked really exhausted and we offered to carry their rifles. Then, if we allowed to do so, we made our way up to the camp where the soldiers were making full use of the Ship Inn and there was a lot of singing going on. It looked very romantic with the field kitchens going, preparing the meals, and the smell of the food, the smell of the horses in the lines, the jingle of the harnesses and the bits, and it made a fourteen year old boy long to be a soldier. No doubt most of these men became part of the original Expeditionary Force that went to France just three years later.

Sometime afterwards some of the first aeroplanes of the Royal Flying Corps flew in along the north sands to Seaton Carew golf links. There were about half-a-dozen of them and they were piloted by young officers; some of the original members of the RFC. At least one of the pilots was killed landing and we were all very sad about this. Later, I saw one officer at close quarters as he was in the barber's shop having a shampoo when I was there. He was quite young and fair and I remember him saying that the sand had got into his hair.

Editor *The incident was more serious than Norman realised. Ten aircraft of No2 Squadron were on their way from Montrose to Salisbury Plain when they halted at Seaton Carew. The next day they took off in bright sunshine but shortly afterwards the aircraft became mired in a thick mist, obscuring all landmarks. Three aircraft crashed and two airmen, a Lieutenant and a mechanic, were killed instantly.*

CHAPTER THREE

A Shilling a Day

The day war broke out, I was thrilled; we were all thrilled. There was a feeling that we were all determined to push the Germans back into Germany. I don't remember any boy saying he didn't want to go, in fact most wanted to get into action before Christmas. We loved our country, patriotism was assumed. We had a great pride in our Empire and I felt I had to defend my country, although looking back now I don't know why I ever joined the army after seeing what shellfire could do. However, I was British and I was fighting for my country, and I think I was in the mood that any guy who was fighting us was a bad guy. Rather silly really, looking back with hindsight; we were all duped to a great extent.

At that time, though, I was proud to be a volunteer who was willing to defend his country and ready to die for his country too. Well, anyway, on the day war broke out, August 4th 1914, I immediately rushed down to the recruiting station in town, told them I was twenty, although I didn't look anything like it. I said I wanted to join a Scottish Regiment and they said that they had vacancies in the King's Own Scottish Borderers, so I enlisted. A local doctor, Dr Robertson, passed me fit for service. This doctor later fought in both wars, was taken prisoner in 1940 and died in captivity.

I had joined up, at least I thought I had. I hadn't told my parents, of course, and the next morning I set off to go down to the station to get on a train to join my Regiment. However, when I got there my father was waiting, with a company director of a firm to which I had recently become an indentured apprentice in the drawing office. The company was Sir William Grey and Company, shipbuilders of Hartlepool, who were building ships for the Royal Navy, as well as shallow draught boats for the River Plate in the Argentine. They told the officer I was already on war work and that, besides, I was only seventeen, 'so I'm afraid you can't have him'. I was embarrassed, of course, and found to my disgust that I was not in the army but rather I was returned to my position as an apprentice. I was, however, given a little badge to put in my lapel to signify that I was on important war work, but for those us who wanted to get into the army this was of limited comfort.

Was it important to feel that I had volunteered rather than waiting, perhaps to be conscripted? Very much so. My word, yes. When conscripts came into the army in 1916, we volunteers had been in for some time,

'Come join the army' A welcoming committee awaits new recruits outside the Drill Hall.

and did not think a great deal of conscripts because they wouldn't have been in France unless they had been compelled to be there.

For nine months I went back to work, until I saw an advertisement in the paper saying that if one went to Stockton-on-Tees one could get a railway ticket to the depot of the regiment one wished to join. I had waited to enlist and, now I was 18, I went and bought a ticket to Stockton on Tees.

Once there I enquired as to which was the most northern regiment in the country, so my parents wouldn't find me easily and take me back home. They said the Rosshire Regiment, the Seaforth Highlanders at Dingwall. I knew a little bit about the Regiment and liked their tartan. They were already fighting in France and had a good history, and when you're joining up you might as well join a good regiment and one that would see some fighting.

I said 'Right, can I have a ticket to go there', so they gave me a ticket and I set off on a Saturday morning, on the 5th June 1915, without telling anyone where I was going, and with just ten shillings in my pocket – one of the new ten-shilling notes. I travelled all day long and by evening I had got as far as Inverness. It was getting late, about 9pm, and I went out into the streets where I came across a lot of Cameron Highlanders, wounded soldiers, who'd been wounded at the Battle of Neuve Chapelle. They were very friendly and asked what I was doing up there, so I told them I'd come to join the army. They said 'Well, you won't get any farther tonight, come along to the Cameron barracks and we'll get a bed for you.' So we went along there and they went into the canteen and asked for the Quartermaster Sergeant to come out. He was a red-faced, beefy looking man with a fierce moustache and he looked at me as the lowest form of life, as no doubt I was to him, and asked what I wanted. He then directed me to go along and get a donkey's breakfast. I didn't know what that was but soon discovered it was a straw mattress and a couple of brown army blankets, so I made a bed and settled down.

These wounded soldiers kept coming in, a little merry, to say the least, from an evening in the town and they were all a little surprised to see a small young stranger in civilian clothes lying on the barrack floor. They kept pushing little flasks of whisky over to me for a swig, but I didn't take any as I had never touched alcohol in my life. I enjoyed talking to them and asked them a few questions before I went to sleep. In the morning I was given a breakfast of porridge and kippers before the Sergeant Major said 'Right, go along to the orderly room and we'll sign you up.' I corrected him saying, 'No, I'm not signing up for the Camerons. I appreciate what you've given me but I've come up here to join the Seaforth Highlanders'. Of course the Seaforths was a rival regiment to the Camerons and he nearly blew his top and told me to get out of there.

I left and went to the railway station where at mid-day I finally got on a train to Dingwall. As it was Sunday evening, few people were about. However, I was directed towards a lodging house where I joined eight other lads from Leeds who were intending to enlist the next day. The lady who ran the house looked at me like I was a babe in arms. I told her I was intending to join the army but I was only small and hardly looked more than a schoolboy, so she gave me two boiled eggs for tea, and scones to feed me up.

The next morning I went down to the drill hall, where I was sworn in by a man wearing a Glengarry with the lovely lyre-shaped tail of a blackcock. He was called Major Manson of the 5th Battalion, and I remember him as a very kind, gentle sort of man. He gave me the king's shilling and the following morning I set off with a small contingent for Fort George on the shores of the Cromarty Firth, on the North Sea. I went through the gates and joined another world. I knew my parents would know perfectly well what I'd done. They knew me.

I was issued with a uniform of sorts, but instead of having a Glengarry I was handed a South African hat turned up at the side: a relic of the Boer War. Instead of a kilt I was given trousers and the rest of a badly fitting uniform. Now in uniform, I had to send my civilian clothes back home, and my mother told me afterwards that she had quite a little weep when she got them. I was not to wear civilian clothes again for a good number of years. Futhermore, apart from the visit of a barber who came from Ardersier, a small village just outside the Fort, I don't think I saw any civilians at all for months.

Fort George was an austere place. The fort itself had a rampart all round it, covered in turf and grass, while underneath there were gaslit dungeon-like quarters. These held about twenty men sleeping on collapsible iron bedsteads, and I was told that that was where I would sleep. They were a pretty rough crowd but they were good fellows. Many had come from Northern Ireland and a number had come from the Western Isles and couldn't even speak English, just Gaelic. They had never seen a railway engine until they had reached the mainland.

The next morning I was detailed to carry the latrine buckets down to the drains to empty them, which I didn't like at all, thinking the job incompatible with my dignity. Afterwards I was sent on to the ramparts to do some drill. The first thing was to double round the top at high speed a couple of times, and then we had ordinary infantry drill overseen by a very young subaltern called Burnham, a handsome man in his officer's uniform. Along with other recruits I did some drill, before Burnham asked if anyone thought they could drill the squad. I stepped forward smartly and said I could, as I had done this at school. So I was given a go and I brought them to attention and called them to number

Fort George pre First World War and today. Almost nothing has changed in the intervening century to the barracks built near Inverness in 1746 after the Jacobite rebellion.

off from the right. As the fourth man called out I stopped him and said, 'As you were', because I had noticed that this was the sort of thing the Drill Sergeant did, he never let them number freely the first time as a matter of discipline. So I called them back and started again with 'and now a little smarter'. You can imagine at eighteen, only 5′ 4½″, I got such black looks from the squad, but then at that age you think you can do anything. I drilled them, changed direction right, changed direction left and managed to get the front rank back into the front rank, before I brought them before the officer. I then stood them to attention and turned around and saluted, handing the platoon back to the officer, who told me to stand them at ease. The officer then walked away with me and said, 'What the hell are you doing here? Why didn't you take a commission?' I told him it took all my time to get into the army at all, never mind as an officer.

That evening Burnham told me to look at the notice board and there I read 'Private W N Collins to be Lance Corporal' and then, in brackets, to be 'unpaid'. I rushed off to the tailor's shop and had one stripe put up, then went to the canteen and ordered a little swagger cane with a silver top. Next morning I walked alongside the chap carrying the latrine buckets, with my cane under my arm, and told him what he could do with them, which pleased me much better!

Being a lance corporal, I was put in charge of a dungeon. I was responsible for issuing the breakfasts, serving from a huge metal tray, bacon, tomatoes and so on, and it was quite a job ensuring that everyone got a fair share. I was a bit unpopular because the ones at the end got short rations. In time I was also made canteen corporal, which meant keeping order in the canteen. I think they chose me because I was a non-drinker. However, I got on very well because I treated the men tactfully, especially those who were drinking heavily.

Norman's third letter after enlistment.

Editor: *On enlistment, Norman was sent to the 3/4th Battalion Seaforth Highlanders, a territorial training battalion formed in April 1915, and made up of new recruits collected at the regiment's depot at Dingwall. This was essentially a second feeder battalion to the 1/4th Territorial Battalion, which had been fighting in France ever since November 1914. It was at that time that any men left behind, combined with new recruits, had created the 2/4th battalion, essentially the first line of drafts to the 1/4th in France. The men of the 2/4th Battalion would therefore be sent abroad before, as Norman reassured his family, those of the 3/4th would necessarily follow.*

The letters and postcards Norman wrote during the 1914-18 war are all now held at the Imperial War Museum, and are divided into six separate files, each a defined period in Norman's war service. The initial two letters were both written on the same day, the first is a letter written shortly after rising in the morning, the second, a hasty plea for much needed materials.

Pte WN Collins No3904
C Company
3/4 Seaforth Highlanders
Fort George Scotland
8th June 1915
Dear Father and Mother

I have found time at last to write you a letter. I am now in Fort George, an old condemned fortress. I stayed with the Cameron Highlanders on Sat. night and Sunday. On Sunday night I went to Dingwall about 40 miles north. I got my uniform there and was billeted at a Sergeant's house with 8 Leeds and Sheffield chaps. We had a fine time. The kit is much better than that of the regulars. We are given

Glengarry hats
Tunic
Trousers
Puttees
2 pairs of thick socks
Pair tan boots
Overcoat (a beauty)
2 pair thick linings
2 shirts
2 towels
Wool helmet
Highland stockings
Red fancy garters
Cardigan wool jacket
Tommy tin and case etc

We are expecting the kilt etc within a few weeks. Up here they are all kilted regiments. I had to pass two doctors up here. Last night we were sleeping on iron bedsteads with two blankets. It is rough but I am enjoying it. We have just got our mattresses or "biscuits" as we call them. When I slept with the Camerons I had a fine time. A mattress and 4 thick blankets. Nearly all the Camerons were wounded at Neuve Chapelle. There are about 1,000 wounded in Inverness. The daily routine of the Seaforths is 6am the pipers wake you up playing "music". Fight your way to the wash basins, wash yourself and keep an eye on your soap (we buy our own).

7am 1st parade drill and run until 8.

Breakfast.

9.15 2nd parade until

12.30 Dinner

2.0 Route march or drill until 4pm

Teas and swim

9.30 in billet

10.00pm pipers play 'lights out'.

Wednesday 7.30 continued.

This morning we go on a route march about 16-20 miles so will not be back until tea: set off at 9.30am. The food is fine, but we are on half rations. Breakfast 3 or 4 kippers or plate ham, tea. Half a loaf of bread to last a day, butter.

Dinner. Meat, potatoes and bread.

Tea. Tinned salmon, jam, cheese, bread, butter, tea.

Will you please send me my pillow and that leather belt with the split ring on. They are both at Hesleden. 2.30pm Just returned from route march. Feel very fit but feet blistered, so please send some boracic powder and a pot of Vaseline for face as the sun will peel it. I haven't received any money yet. The commissioned officers are fine but we have some awful sergeants from India.

Evening 8 June 1915

Will you send the things in a tin box so that I can keep my soap and shaving outfit in it etc. 50% of this battalion are Irish. They are big thieves. A quarter are English and the rest Scots. I feel as fit as a top. Marching thro' fine woods etc. We get 1 shilling a day but will have to have 6d of that for food as we have to buy supper, 4d and anything we want to drink after dinner. We are not allowed out of the fortress except with the regiment so we can buy nothing as the nearest village, about three miles away, is out of bounds and if we were caught there it would mean a week's pay stopped. Here are a lot of things I need.

1 padlock

1 boot brush and polish

Vaseline
Boracic powder
Needle and cotton
Black wool
Piece of looking glass
Polish for buttons.

I believe I returned some gloves, if so please send them. I don't suppose I will get any leave for 3 months and then it will just be a weekend so I will not be able to get home. It is a proper regiment and doesn't play at soldiers and will make a man of me.

Well 'Ta Ta! the noo' as the natives say here. I will write every week. The regulars here who have been to the front from the beginning think it will all be over in 3 months.

Your loving son
Norman

9th June 1915
Dear Bolton
How are you blowing? The country up here is lovely.....I have been on a route march today for about 12 miles. We have a fine band, 4 pipers and drummers etc. The bagpipes have a wonderful effect when you feel tired. The fortress itself is an awful hole. I hope we get moved soon. The only shop we can go to is the barbers.

Can you send me notepaper and postcards as I haven't much money to buy them and a 'London Opinion' or two. I haven't seen a paper this week also please send my pipe as I am not going to buy cigarettes.

The officers here are gentlemen. I am billeted with some Leeds chaps, decent chaps. Inverness is a fine town. I think I will go there when I get a couple of day's leave. It is rumoured that we are going to England to train...

Ta Ta! More drill tomorrow
Best Love Norman.

Friday 8.30 YMCA Tent, Camerons Camp. 11.6.15 (Postcard)
Dear Bolton
How goes it? I am in full war rig. Tartan kilt, red and white stockings etc. I think I will get permission from the C.O to go to the village and have my photo taken. We are not allowed to go more than 1 mile from the fort, and we are miles from anywhere. I have put 30 hours drill in up to now. Fit as a top. Please write soon.

We have heard there has been an air raid in Hull. Please send me a paper.

Nairn is 10 miles from here. Scenery lovely.

June 12th. Sat. 3.30pm

Dear Father and Mother

I have just received your letter. It was very welcome. I will just give you my weeks 'work', then you will have an idea what life in the army is like.

Arrived in Inverness 9.0pm. Saturday and was taken to the barracks by a wounded Cameron. The sergeant gave me a bed and I slept with my trousers on. Most of the men in the room were recovering from wounds. Next morning a Leeds chap lent me soap and towel and I had a wash. For breakfast I had tea, ham, bread and butter. Then I spent an hr or so picking the blanket fluff off my trousers.

Then I walked along the banks of the Loch Ness and on to the Islands. There are about half-a-dozen small islands covered with trees and spanned by trellis-work bridges. On each side of the Loch the hills rise, covered with pine trees etc and lovely villas and cottages and snow on the summits. The sea birds are so tame that they will perch within a few feet of people. I wasn't very hungry so I just had a glass of lemonade and a few biscuits for dinner and had a walk round. I then got a train for Dingwall. Next morning I [enlisted and] was given my uniform all but the kilt. (We are supplied with trousers or 'trews' as they are called). I saw the army tailors making kilts. A full kilt had 16 yards of tartan in it at 6 shillings per yard. The kilts now have only about 9 yards in them. The tartan is blue, green, red and white, with a sporran of black and white horse hair. Red and white stockings and khaki spats. On Monday afternoon I was playing football then we were marched down to the station carrying our kit-bags weighing about 80lbs. Arrived Fort George about 7pm. We were too late for tea so we went down to the canteen (teetotal) and had potatoes and sausage 4d with a bottle of lemonade. We are sleeping in bomb-proof cells in the fort. I didn't sleep much that night as we had no mattresses. Tuesday, the pipers played at 6am, parade at 7. For an hr we run around the ramparts to give us an appetite for breakfast. Every day a man is made 'orderly' for his room and has to bring in the breakfast, dinner and tea and wash up for the men in his room. He has also to sweep out the room.

Breakfast at 8, then polish your buttons. Parade at 9. We are taken outside the fort and drilled on the moor with about 1000 men, until 12.30. Every day it has been blazing hot.

Dinner at 1pm. Parade again at 2pm. Drill or swim until 4pm then finish for the day. It is very monotonous at night as we are not allowed near the village. On Wednesday we went for a route march into the country for about 15 miles. Today we have just been for another one and we marched back thro' the nearest village of Ardersier. What a relief it was to see a civilian again, for I have not seen one since coming to the Fort. Every night the pipers play 'lights out' at 10pm. What an easy time the

'English' regiments have. Going to theatres etc. I prefer being here tho', the air is so healthy. My face is beginning to peel with the sun, and I have never felt so well before. The food isn't bad but some days we do not get sufficient while today we had too much and had to waste a lot. One thing I miss badly is fruit. We never see it as there are no shops to buy it. I could do with a tin of fruit salts every week, to make up for it. Every day is much alike. The officers are very nice. Our commanding officer has risen from the ranks and his nephew is my Corporal. He lends me his kilt to go swanking up to the Y.M.C.A tent in the Cameron Highlander's camp. There is great rivalry between the two clans. There are only 3 of us in our room who can claim any Scotch relations and only one next door out of 30 men. The others are Leeds. Their awful Yorkshire 'twang' gets on my nerves. They go 'in't' or 'tit' or always do a thing 'right' well. I will write twice a week, Sunday and Wednesday. I was drilling 20 men the other day. I have just been up to the Quarter-Master's room getting an enamelled plate and mug and he gave me two new bath towels. You might send me 2 or 3 sweat rags for washing up. Also some of that tape with my initials on. I think you get it at any drapers. We were paid yesterday. I got 4 shillings. I will need to buy stamps, boot polish, brass polish and supper out of this for the week so I will not be able to send any home this week. Supper is 6d (2 slices bread 1d, potatoes and sausage 4d, lemonade 1d).

It is surprising how warm the kilt is. It is a little strange at first having no trousers on, but the kilt is far more comfortable. Our 2/4ths are sleeping on the ground without tents. At the front the men have no blankets, only waterproof sheets. It is very strange that we can see snow while we are roasting in the sun. Church parade tomorrow. I am going to the Presbyterian church. A mouth organ would be very useful. I have received 2 parcels of

After his first promotion; Norman as an 18 year-old lance corporal.

45

papers and 2 letters.

If I had not been perfectly fit I would never have got into this regiment as the [medical] examination is very strict. Two chaps in our room were passed in Ireland and rejected here. I passed the eyesight not very well without glasses. After 2 months I think we are given a free pass for 7 days. In about a month's time I am going to try and get two days' leave and go to Inverness with my corporal.

I would like to come and see you but of course it is too far. I will not touch alcoholic drinks at all.

Well 'Ta-Ta the noo

Your loving son Norman

Sunday 7.0pm
20th June/15
Dear Father, Mother, and Bolton
I hope you are all keeping well. Are any of my letters and cards reaching home? The last word I received from Hesleden was 9 days ago, a week gone Sat. I have been here a fortnight and so far have got one letter from Bolton and one from Father.

A middle-aged recruit undergoes a medical examination. Early on in the war the army could afford to be selective until the number of willing volunteers began to dry up.   IWM Q30062

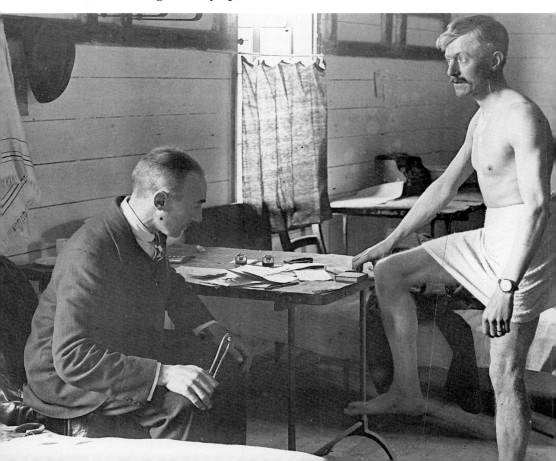

Thank you very much for the Daily Mails, London Opinion etc. On Saturday I sent off a Seaforth sporran and a cap. They are my own and you may keep them, also the towel. The cap requires a good wash and new ribbon. If it is of no use burn it and keep the badge. Please let me know by letter if you receive them, not on an open card. I got them from a chap going to France in another battalion of Seaforths. Altogether I have four towels like that one. This week we were supplied with a razor, brush, toothbrush, comb in a hold-all; some canvas shoes. All our dirty clothing etc is washed for 3d a week. My shoes cost 4 shillings to mend. Every day we get more than we can eat. Every Sunday we have tinned fruit. Please send my bank-book off and let me know. If you take the number off it, it can't go astray. I have been on 7 route marches, a total distance of over 100 miles. The big chaps always knock up first. They often faint with the sun. It is laughable to see some chaps hopping along, I saw one chap crawling on his hands and knees. I have never felt fitter and my feet are quite hard. My face has nearly completely peeled. The skin comes off in chunks. Fred Chiverton sent me a lot of books yesterday. Every week we scrub the room out and it is closely inspected by the Colonel. What I don't know about washing floors, greasy pots etc isn't worth knowing. We are not allowed to sit down to meals except in full dress. Can you send me anything that will take stains off cloth (grease stains). Our rifles make a mess of our shoulder straps...

On Sundays I attend drum-head service with the Presbyterians. All the Englishmen here are Church of England or Roman Catholics. We are not allowed out of the Fort until 5pm and then limited to a mile. Of course we are training all day on the moors and do not feel like doing much walking afterwards. One day is very much like another. We have a boy of sixteen in our room and an old soldier of fifty-five. I don't know how they got in. The 'General' as we call him is a useful old chap and has served about 20 years in the army. He looks after the hot baths and for a 'pint' he will have the water boiling and the bath scrubbed out. Every night he has from 8 to 10 pints of beer yet he is never in the least drunk.

It is a great mistake to think that the Highlanders are tall men. As a rule they are about 5 foot 6 or 7 inches, average height and stockily built. Not one in 100 are 6 feet high in all regiments I've seen.

If you will write once a week it will be very welcome. I got the Daily Mail tonight that was posted on the 19th. Fred Chiverton tells me that 50 people were killed by Zeppelins in Newcastle.

Well there is no more news except that it will be a long time before I get tired of this life. I am looking forward to drill etc tomorrow.

Will you send me 2 or 3 tins of Cold Cream as if the blisters on my face burst they will leave marks. Some chaps' faces are full of small holes with blisters. Ta Ta!

With best love Norman

I haven't come across a mean Scotchman yet. The Yorkshire men are very mean.

I was pulled up the other night for having one hand in my trouser pocket!

July 1 1915 Thursday 8.30
Dear Bolton
Just received your letter. Thank you very much. I don't know whether I will be promoted any more. You see I am so little and young compared with some of these chaps. Tho' my squad is the best drilled in the company we are never singled out to be the 'awkward squad'. If a squad blunders it is sent to 'form fours' and right turn etc for 2 or 3 hours and is called the 'A.S.' I am getting quite a 'voice'. 'Double up! Double up! Left right! Left right!' etc. My throat is very sore to night with shouting. I have[n't] fired on the range yet, but have used blanks to learn rapid loading and firing and I am now on with bayonet fighting. There is a lot

Recruits practise a bayonet charge.   IWM Q53752

of work about a service rifle, it holds from 6-11 cartridges and is very heavy. At first I could hardly lift one with one hand. We learn sighting and rifle drill. I am also getting lessons in bayonet work. It is great, tho' very tiring. Right guard, lunge etc. We learn to fight men on horseback. It is surprising but the man with the bayonet can nearly always get his man. It is a very deadly weapon...

Thank you for the papers. I have been very seedy up to today, never had so much pain in my life thro' these terrible germs the doctor injected into me. Inoculation costs [the army] about 10 guineas tho' and prevents fever. Well ta ta old cock for the present. Walking in a kilt at first is just like going to the office with nothing but your boots, shirt and jacket on and a belt round the middle. After a route march we are covered with dust from the waist downwards, as we sweat and the dust clings.

Rather draughty as well.

Best love Norman.

Undated
Thursday 3.30pm
Dear all

A column of Argyll and Sutherland Highlanders wends its way through the Scottish countryside. Frequent and exhausting route marches quickly made recruits extremely fit.

Just received your welcome parcel. Everything in it is good. It has come very quickly you will notice. I don't suppose you would have received my letter until this morning. I have just come off coal parade. We N.C.O.s have an easy time on Thursday afternoon, just looking after the privates carrying coal.

We have some very inexperienced officers. I could teach a lot of them how to drill. We have one who is 6 foot 6 inches high and as thin as a lath. His legs are no thicker than my arm and he does look funny in the kilt. He knows nothing about drill. A lot of chaps here have applied for a commission and some can hardly spell their own names and are very uneducated. I might have a try myself as I think I would have a very good chance if I could get some one to speak for me. This morning it was raining heavily and we did not go on parade until 10 o'clock, so I had the room scrubbed out and the tables and forms scrubbed. They are nice and white now. I have just enjoyed a banana. Up here the fruit is very dear. A cart comes near the Fort once a week with oranges etc. An orange is 2d and bananas 2d each! Here lemonade is 2d a bottle. A loaf of bread is 4d in all the villages. I think this is on account of the cost [of] railway freights so far north. Yesterday we were on a route march with full kit. Valise, haversack, trenching tool, bayonet sheath, water bottle ammunition pouches etc. We look something like this:

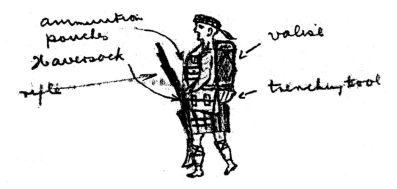

6.0pm I have just had a swim and then my tea. The boracic powder is fine for keeping the feet dry on the march.

Yesterday about 3000 'kilties' marched to Perth. They will take about 4 days to get there. A 4/4th Seaforths has been commenced at Dingwall so we are expecting to move soon. I hope so as it is rather monotonous here. There is no more news at present. I am in the best of health and hope you all are.

With best love Norman.

July 1st 1915 Thursday 7.30

Dear all at the cottage

I have been ill this week and am just about better now. I was delirious for about 24 hours thro' being inoculated. Altho' fully dressed even with shoes on and in bed with blankets and overcoat. I couldn't keep warm. It is a good thing to be inoculated and I am quite well again and fever proof.

I am on bayonet fighting. It is fine. A rifle and bayonet is nearly as long as myself and very heavy. It is fine being an NCO. No more duty work, coal parade or washing floors.

Yesterday there were some sports here and I managed to get there although I felt really shaky. On Tuesday I couldn't lift a cup of tea. The finest sight I have ever seen was 20 pipers and 10 drummers in full Seaforth uniform marching up and down the field with their sporrans and kilt flying, plaids etc and what a row they made! The pipes do stir the blood.

With best love Norman

July 11th 1915

Dear mother

I enclose a postcard of the prison here which I was in charge of from 9am Friday until 9am Saturday. I was Corporal of the Guard and had 3 privates with me (all been wounded in France). Each private has 2 hours on sentry-go for 24 hours. My job was to put in prison any drunken men who came in late and let in any motor-cars etc and change the sentries every 2 hours. I also saw that they were washed and shaved, and took them for a walk with two privates with fixed bayonets each side. At night I hadn't to sleep of course and we are not allowed to remove our belts or bayonets. Yesterday I got another new kilt. You see I am a 'pal' of the Quarter Master and he got some fine kilts in with box pleats instead of the ordinary pleats, so I 'swapped' my 'old' one. It is much warmer and has about 7 yards of cloth in it. Did I tell you that I have a full English uniform as well as the highland one? I wear this on such things as coal fatigue or any rough work. It is surprising what a lot of trouble they take over our dress in war time.

Best love Norman

PS Monday. Will you please send me some strong disinfectant soap and some Keatings. Some of the chaps here are not clean. I am sending home my flannel to be washed and disinfected. I think I will send my washing home every week as it is not done properly here, just dipped in and out and it is always wet when we get it. Will you send my other flannel and two thin cotton shirts as they are far healthier and prevent 'livestock'. I will send the shirts I have here in exchange for the cotton ones. If you can send me some stuff that will prevent and get rid of lice etc I will be much obliged as they are fairly common here. Norman.

'Stirring the blood'. The pipes could quickly re-invigorate the step of tired men on the march.

Undated

Dear Bolton

I have just got word that I am to be Orderly Corporal for the rest of today. It is an awful job. I have to see that every one in 'C' Company gets his food, and I am the postman and have to deliver perhaps 100 or more letters and parcels.... The book on infantry is very useful; we are now doing a lot of extended order drill 'skirmishing' and we work by signals.... It is very interesting. We run a few yards then drop down flat on the ground and practise crawling for any little hollow in the ground. We drill behind the rifle range and are used to the 'whine' of the bullets. If a bullet misses the target it goes over our heads and they are sometimes uncomfortably near.

.....I wouldn't advise you to join any of these Corps such as the Royal Army Medical Corps or Army Service Corps where eyesight tests are not needed. It is very rough work. We have clerks here who use typewriting, shorthand etc. We could do with a few 'business men' to look after the pay. They make an awful mess of it here. We get shillings stopped off our pay and no one has any idea why. We are supposed to get 1 shilling per day (private) and Lance Corporal 1/3 and yet I have usually got 6 shillings and sometimes 4 shillings a week.

Best love Norman.

PS 7.0pm just fed 204 men and delivered their letters, at 8.0 I have to look after their suppers.

Since last week we have got 4 meals a day instead of 3. It is a new order. We got a cup of coffee and some cheese. The cheese is well trained. If you shout 'quick march' it walks off the table!

We have got our full kit. It weighs about 90lbs with the rifle. There's a valise in which we carry overcoat, tommy tins, knife and fork, spoon, 2 shirts, 2 pairs socks, boots, shoes etc, a haversack at one side for food etc, 2 big pouches for 150 rounds of ammunition, one each side, a trenching tool for digging ourselves in if wounded, bayonet and case, water bottle etc and rifle. It is like harnessing a horse to dress. We do not take blankets to France, just sleep on the ground. Ta ta Norman

22-7-15 Thursday 9.45am
Dear Bolton
Yesterday our battalion marched to Nairn and back with full kit. You will see it on the map. We set off at 9.15am and arrived at 12.15. Then we had a pie and a bottle of lemonade and half an hour's rest and marched back at 4.30pm. I was rather unlucky for I was in charge of the A.S.C. guard that night (about a mile away from the Fort) and so had just time for something to eat and a wash then on duty again at 6.30 until 8am this morning. We go on guard with full kit (including rifle and bayonet). There are 3 men in our room off parade with bad feet after the march. The first lieutenant of our company has just been enquiring how I feel after a long march and 13 hours' duty immediately after.

Well, about getting a commission. On Monday our C.O. called me out on parade and we had a long talk. He asked where I had been educated, what my trade was and if I was old enough to take up a commission. He said he could see that I was different to the other recruits and complimented me on the neatness of some reports that I had written for him. He said that I was a d[amned]fool for enlisting as a private as I was not in my right place in the ranks. He only had 7 weeks' training before going to the front and he told me all about how to get a commission and the cost of everything. I promised him I would apply for one and he told me to hurry up about it. The Government allowance is £50 and in an English regiment the kit only costs from £20 to £30. In a Highland regiment it costs about £50 so he advised me to try the Durham Light Infantry or the Royal Field Artillery or the Royal Garrison Artillery.

I have written to Uncle Tom about it and have asked him to obtain the names of the COs of any of the Durham or Yorkshire Territorials. Next to

Preparing for physical training or 'Swedish Drill' as it was known.

a Highland Regiment I prefer a Cavalry, Yeomanry or Royal Field Artillery. I will be sorry to say goodbye to the kilt though. With my engineering and Technical College training I ought to get on well in the R.F.A.

In a fortnight's time 'A' Company leaves for France. They have only had 11 weeks to 16 weeks' training and have had no leave. Before going they will get 4 days. 'C' Company goes either the last week in August or early in September. (I asked the C.O.).

We have had our bonny red and white stockings taken away and been given khaki ones. In the trenches we pull them up above the knee at night. They are very long. The tartan kilt is hidden by a khaki apron and the cap by a khaki cover. The reason we go out so quickly is because the 4th Seaforths have only about 300 men at the front out of about 1,500.

I am quite content here as an N.C.O. tho' it would be much better as an officer. As far as education goes I am sure I will do. I am good at mathematics, algebra, trigonometry, writing etc. There are several second lieutenants that I know who haven't had much education. Some of the N.C.O.s here who have applied could not write the application form out.

I think a person who has roughed it as a private makes a better officer and understands the men better than one straight from school. The Highland training is very good too. We have been thro' everything

Nairn: 'Brighton of the north' according to Norman.

practically while the majority of Kitchener's army know nothing of rifle drill or bayonet fighting. Thank you for the paper.

The man that took my photo knew nothing about it when I went for it, so I had them taken again on Sunday. They will be ready today but I will get them tomorrow when I get paid and will send them straight away. There are no professional photographers within 12 miles of here so I don't suppose they will be very good.

I will close now... Best love to all. Norman.

Tuesday

Dear all

...We have to be very careful about changing our shirts at least once a week, as with sweating every day a peculiar kind of 'livestock' develops if a person wears the same underclothing for a fortnight. I have a bath twice a week. At the front all the officers and men are infested with millions of creepers and it's impossible to keep clear of them.

An order came out yesterday that everyone must grow a moustache. If we shave our upper lip we will get Guard-room! I hope you'll recognise me when I return.

Best love Norman

Sunday 10.00am

Dear mother

....I was at Inverness yesterday for about two hours (5pm to 7pm) had a good tea in a café and bought a few presents.

There are some lovely tartan novelties here and I could spend pounds on them. I had a look in the 'Clan-Tartan Warehouse' and it looks very novel to one who isn't used to seeing kilts, tartan bonnets, sporrans etc instead of trousers and bowlers.

I hope you will like the socks, Bolton, they are the real Mackenzie (Seaforth) tartan. The Seaforths are composed of several clans, Mckrays, Urquharts, Mackenzie, Mcleans, Macdonalds etc and the Mackenzie tartan was chosen as the Regimental tartan. Collins is a real scotch name (Edinburgh district) and Norman is real Highland.

I would like to spend six months' holiday touring the Highlands. There are reindeer, wild-cats, Golden eagles etc in the woods.

With best love Norman

Nairn Sat 6.30pm

Dear all

I am having an afternoon's holiday here. This is a bonny place and is called 'the Brighton of the north' as it is a popular health resort for the English visitors (you see I am seeing the world free of charge).

I have just seen our draft away to France. It is the first from 'C' Company. A lot of my chums have gone and a lot more just had six weeks' training. They had the trains chalked with notices such as 'First stop Berlin'. When an officer goes to the Front he wears the same equipment as a private and carries a rifle and bayonet but not sword or leather belt.

...It is wonderful how fit we keep as if our clothes are wet we let them dry on us and after washing anything we sleep on it. This is the correct way in the army! It was three months yesterday since I last slept in a bed.

I am writing in a 'working men's club' paper, pen, envelope free. Scotch people are the best I have ever met. When we are marching through woods we often see old women of about 80 gathering wood. Some try to dance to the time of the pipes and some start to weep. They do look picturesque though with their tartan shawls.

Sunday 1pm (still at Nairn). We decided to stay overnight here and so were recommended to go to a Temperance Hotel by the ladies who look after this Club. It was fine to sleep in a bed again and have our shoes brushed for us and have ham and eggs for breakfast. My chum (Jock Macgregor) was inoculated on Friday as he is going to France in a fortnight's time and so we are having a week-end together. I have just have been introduced to a lady called Thompson from Sutherland. Her brother works in the National Provincial Bank at Hartlepool and was in the house next to the one in which the Salvation Army Captain was killed during the bombardment. I happened to have a photograph of the very house with me. [Ed. *see page 19 bottom*] This was a curious co-incidence meeting each other so far north. ...Could you send me a set of views of the bombardment as people are very interested about it here.

With best love Norman

Sunday Fort George

Dear all

I've had a very quiet weekend, just eating and sleeping. The life seems to suit me as I now weigh 10st 8lbs in uniform and that belt you sent when I first joined won't go around my waist. I haven't grown any taller but have the thickest leg in 'C' Company and am the youngest.

All the men who joined when I did go on furlough on Tuesday for a week as they have fired their Trained Man's Course. I am not entitled to one as I was kept back to drill recruits. They all go to the Front when they come off leave. We have 35 officers in the battalion and there are only about 500 men left. When I joined we had only about 6 officers. There are about 6 applications for commissions waiting to be signed by the C.O. mine amongst them. I am quite content as I am at present as I am learning a lot and often act as a subaltern in command of a platoon. When I get a commission I will know my job thoroughly. It is amusing to see the new officers try and drill a squad. They are very nervous and many a time I give them a hint what to do. They are decent fellows though; that is the majority...

We have an old reprobate in our room, an old soldier of about 55, one John Stubbs. We dress him carefully on a Saturday and he goes off to the village of Inverness for the day. At night he comes rolling in and we undress him and put him to bed, fill his pipe and light it and keep him quiet so that he doesn't get guard room. He can drink 12 pints of beer without rolling at all.

Yesterday I was forced to put a man in the guard-room for insubordination. It isn't a nice job but had to be done as an army is no use without discipline. He will be tried tomorrow.

With best love, Norman

Monday, another draft picked today of 60 men to go out on Wednesday, as they are needed urgently. If I had had my leave I would have had to go. Been bayonet fighting today. Sticking sacks.

Monday Fort George

Dear all

....Did I tell you of the burglaries? About six weeks ago there were watches, pocket books, razors, belts, money, and dozens of articles to the value of about £30 missing. The chap that sleeps next to me had a pocket book taken out of his box. One morning a chap was seen walking on the sea shore outside the Fort, with a jam tin in his hand and was arrested for being off parade. The tin was full of watches, jewellery etc the spoil of the day's raid. His box was full of stolen articles and also a hoard was discovered under the floor in his room. He was sentenced to about four months' hard labour and discharged from the service. I think he got off very easily.

A fortnight ago a young Irishman of about 18 years (in our room) deserted but was caught about 40 miles past Inverness. He meant to walk to Ireland over the Grampian Mountains. He would probably have lost his way and not been heard of again if he hadn't been captured, or perhaps become a hermit and let his hair grow.

I will be about the oldest trained soldier when we move as the rest have gone or are going to France.

With best love, Norman

Tuesday
...A draft went last week and another goes August 14. Today the draft was chosen for September. We commence the musketry exam on Monday so I will try for the last week in August at home. ...I was at Inverness on Saturday afternoon at some sports. Uncle Tom is sending me a note from Colonel Robson to show the C.O. when I get my form signed. The Royal Engineers unit is up to full strength so I will try for the infantry as I am trained for that.

In three weeks' time I will have passed through the full course of training and be a 'trained soldier'. I think we are to get the new style of short rifle. Up to now the Seaforths have fought with the old Lee-Enfield with the short bayonet.

Best love, Norman

12/9/15 Fort George 15th Week
Sunday 9.30am
Dear all
This week we have had lovely weather. I was glad to hear that the Zeps hadn't been to Hartlepool. I thought they had as London Opinion, John Bull etc didn't arrive. Every week these papers have come punctual to the minute. All the June and part of the July recruits are on furlough this week as they go to France next week. I am amongst the dozen who are left. Yesterday I turned the scale at 11 stone, in the kilt, so you see I am not wasting away with hard training. Those stories about the British Army being badly fed are not true, at least they do not apply to Highland

regiments. ...I was made a full corporal but when it was known that I have an application for a commission in, it was taken from me. ....We are getting a lot of Zeppelin alarms for practice. It is usually when we have gone to sleep and are very unwilling to turn out of bed. The bugles sound the alarm and in three minutes we are lined up and marched on to the parade ground. Then the whole battalion and also the regulars are marched out of the Fort through the main gate (about 6 feet wide) and onto the common where we scatter and lie down on our faces. Of course we always had the usual fire alarms but were not marched outside the Fort. We have often been turned out in the pouring rain at 12 midnight.

Best love, Norman

Sunday 19/9/15

Dear all

I wrote on the Monday morning and meant to post it but I wasn't very well and had to go to the hospital. I think it is with drinking bad water, as my throat was black. All last week my temperature was buzzing about 103° but today I am about normal and go on solid food tomorrow. I've had milk and soda last week and couldn't swallow and at present am very hungry. When I get a leave home I will only get about an hour's notice so may only be able to give you the same notice, so have all the grub ready. The dinner I am looking forward to is: rabbit pie with ham and eggs in and plenty of brown crust and mashed potatoes. I haven't seen a peeled or mashed potato since I became a Seaforth. Our cooks spoil the food. I've seen 40 or 50 cabbages thrown away by the men as they were served up raw and stores of ham and meat thrown away half raw. Luckily I have good teeth and can handle most things. The quality of the food is the best possible but we have amateur men cooks.

There is a possibility of me getting about three days' leave after being ill so don't be surprised if I am sitting on the step when you come back from gathering firewood.

Best love, Norman

Editor: *It is clear from the following letter that Norman was given home leave, although if he received just the three days he was predicting, he could barely have arrived home for more than a few hours before undertaking the long journey back to Fort George.*

26.9.15

Dear all

When I arrived [Fort George] I walked through the worst rain and hail storm I have ever seen. It is pouring down now and had been on 24 hours without a stop. The water went through my puttees and stockings and my boots were full of water. Lights were out when I got to the Fort and I had

Men of the Scottish Rifles spar outside their barracks. Norman practised the pugilist's art with the brother of the champion boxer Billy Wells.

to borrow matches. Someone had collared my bed and blankets so I had to find one and make a bed and undress in the dark. My bed consisted of one blanket and a wet overcoat with my tunic for a pillow. I ate a wet rabbit pie in the dark and enjoyed it, then had as sound a sleep as I've ever had until 4.30 this morning. A chum of mine here has just got a letter from France (his brother is Sergeant Major in the 4th Seaforths) and he says that we have bombarded the lines for four days and hope to commence an advance when the guns cease. [Ed. a *reference to the Battle of Loos*]

Best love, Norman

28/9/15
Dear all

There have been no letters to the Fort this week as about six bridges have been swept away and a lot of roads flooded by the storm. We have sent a fatigue party of 100 men to help repair them. One bridge is south of the Grampians and one between here and Inverness, also the Inverness road is flooded. Two bridges farther north have also gone. My train was the last one to cross them. It is impossible to go to Inverness or Edinburgh so if I had stayed over the weekend I would have perhaps had a fortnight at home. The weather is very cold here. Yesterday we paraded in a heavy hail storm. Hail as big as peas. I drew 23/- in money yesterday. I received 1/9 a day ration money for the four days' leave besides my pay for a fortnight. For the time in hospital 7d a day was deducted. It is a shame that they stop that as the wounded men who are making an allowance to their wives are in debt as the Government allows the wife about 12/6 and the man also 3/6 out of his 7/- a week, so if he is in the hospital he is charged 4/- a week and only draws 3/6. I have seen cases in *John Bull* where a man has been discharged unfit after six months in the hospital and when he has claimed six months' pay has been told that he is over £1 in debt. The allowance stops when he is discharged. Funny thing the army. A man who was in hospital when I was remarked what a fine time he was going to have when he drew his wages for three months (he expected about £5) and got a shock when I explained that he owed the Government about 7/- instead.

We were expecting a big advance in France last week. Two boys were drowned here after the route march on Wednesday. Both under age. Very strong currents in the Firth. I will be very careful.

Best love, Norman

Editor: *It seems palpably unfair that a man who, through no fault of his own, should have his pay docked when in hospital. It was not a meanness peculiar to the forces: merchant seamen whose ships sank at sea also lost their pay once they were cast adrift. The thinking was, in both cases, that once the soldier was incapacitated or the sailor had lost his ship, neither could perform the job for which he was being paid.*

October 15, Thursday 9.00pm QMS Office
Dear all
.....It is dark very soon now and I don't know how we will put the winter in here as there are no amusements at all. Hesleden is a frivolous place compared with the Fort. There are no lights here except in the rooms. We have a church in the Fort and two schools for the children and band boys. There is a burial place for the Regiment pets and all have headstones stating their histories. The last dog was in India, Malta, South Africa and Fort George.

Did I ever tell you that Bombadier Wells' brother is in our battalion? I know him very well and have boxed with him. He is 18 years of age and is six feet high and is the image of his brother Billy, same style in boxing.

He often seconds me. He was wounded in seven places at Neuve Chapelle

On Friday I saw our C.O. about my papers. The silly ass had signed them but doesn't know what he has done with them. He advised me to get attached to a unit and make out fresh papers (Territorial).

Editor: 'Bombardier' Billy Wells (1889-1967) was the great white hope of British heavyweight boxing, in the years leading up to and including the First World War. Champion of Britain, he successfully defended the title thirteen times. Among his fifty-four fights between 1910 and 1925 were those against the famous black boxer and future world champion, Jack Johnson, and the French heavyweight Georges Carpentier. Bombardier Wells is also remembered for being the man who banged the gong at the start of the J Arthur Rank Films in the 1930s and '40s.

Sunday

I couldn't get an interview with the C.O. so will have to wait until he decides to sign my papers. If he had signed them in August I would have had my commission within a month, the 10th Seaforth (Kitchener's Army) need officers. I hope the C.O. has not lost my papers. He treated the Quarter Master Sergeant very shabbily. The Q had a commission practically in the Sussex Rifles. The C.O. of the Rifles accepted him as a 1st Lieutenant and was putting his papers through when our C.O. offered the QS a commission in this regiment so the first was cancelled but he has not sent his papers in yet and he should have had his commission two months ago.

If I do not hear any more about my papers when I get to Ripon (they may easily be lost in moving) do you think I should apply again to the 10th Seaforths?

Sunday [one week later]

I will be home in three weeks as I am now on with my musketry course and will be a trained man when I finish it and will be given seven days' leave, pending overseas draft. My papers for a commission were signed by the Major a long time ago but I will have to finally have an interview with a Brigadier General at Cromarty. I am to see the Major tomorrow to see when I can get this interview.

Wednesday

I will be home on Monday for six or eight days. I have not been on parade this week as I was inoculated on Monday afternoon. The C.O. sent for me yesterday and had about half an hour talk. He has signed my papers for this regiment and written to the Brigadier General asking for an interview as early as possible. In Kitchener's Army it is not necessary to see anyone above your commissioning officer. I don't know why it is more difficult in the Territorial Force. My papers are sent to the War Office next week, I will be gazetted within three weeks from now.

With best love, Norman

Norman

In the autumn of 1915, we moved down to Ripon and I was very pleased about this because I had some relations who lived there, an aunt, uncle and two cousins, and I visualised the possibility of popping round for something different to eat. We came from an isolated fort in the north of Scotland to a very well populated army camp that held many thousands of men. There we lived in army huts with a much better social life altogether.

LCpl WN Collins 9304 C Coy
3/4 Seaforths No2 Camp
No3 Brigade South Camp Ripon
5 November 1915
Dear All
Arrived Ripon 7.30am Wednesday. Left Fort 4.45pm.

Very muddy here but much better than the Fort. We are allowed into the town after 5.30pm. I never thought 2 years ago that the next time I crossed the river at Ripon would be behind the bag-pipes without trousers on.

I will probably be able to get home occasionally.

Our musketry party will be delayed some time as the range here is not ready yet. The nearer Christmas the better.

Love Norman.

(undated)
Dear all
I am writing this from 'Cader Idris' [Ed. *the home of his aunt and uncle*]. Aunty Edie, Uncle George etc have gone to church and I have just had a hot bath. It is playing at soldiers, being at Ripon. I enclose a territorial form and would like Mr Bell to sign it or could Col. Robson? There are thousands of kilties in Ripon. Seaforths, Gordons, Black Watch, Camerons; and the Argyll & Sutherland Highlanders come tomorrow. The Seaforth uniform beats the rest easily. I will try to get home for next week-end. The huts here are very comfortable and have electric light installation.

You might send my sporran to Auntie Edie's as this is a different place to Fort George. I passed through Hartlepool on my way to Ripon. The

South Camp, Ripon, where the Seaforths moved in the autumn of 1915.

troop train left Fort George about 4.45pm and arrived here at 7.30am. We only stopped at Perth, Edinburgh, Newcastle and Stockton but weren't allowed to leave the train from the Fort to Ripon. It snowed coming over the Grampians. As the range isn't ready here it will be some time before I can apply for 7 days leave. The range is 4 miles from camp. We are allowed in the town on Saturdays and Sundays after 2pm and during the week after 5pm. The English soldiers here don't show up very well against the kilties.

No more news so ta! ta! the noo, Norman

(undated)

Dear all

Hope you are all well. I only have another 35 shots to fire and will then be inoculated and get 7 days' furlough, so hope to be home early next week. Will you get my birth certificate ready. I am writing Uncle Tom to see if he can get me a replica of Col. Robson's recommendation as the C.O. lost the other with my papers. I haven't any time to waste now as 'C' Coy is being broken up and my Captain who will do anything he can to assist me is being transferred to another company on Saturday, also another draft is going out before Christmas and I am available for it.

If you can possibly do it I would like you to send the papers, birth certificate and recommendation this week.

The rifle range is 4 miles away from camp. It is very cold firing in the snow, and must be very cold in Scotland.

Will you send me the mail thro' occasionally as I like news of Hartlepool. The people here seem to pity us going abroad with bare knees in this weather.

No more news so will close with love Norman.

P.S. Thanks for sporran etc. Send papers to Aunty Edie's. If there is any possibility of obtaining the recommendation from Col. Robson please wait for it.

Wed

Dear all

I have just received the papers. You will have also received my letter of this morning [previous letter] asking for them. Tomorrow I will finish my musketry on the range, then there will be a field day and inoculation so that I will probably be home on Monday.

If they do not inoculate us until after our furlough I may be home on Sat, so I think you had better not come this week-end as I am unsettled.

If Uncle Tom can get that recommendation please send it as soon as possible. We are sending a draft away before Christmas. Thank Mr Bell for signing the papers. You forgot to enclose my birth certificate. I am sorry that my Captain has been transferred (tonight) to another company as I don't know the new one, and I must apply through my company officer. If I get the recommendation it will carry weight with him I suppose.

This is the first time this week I have been out of camp as I have been so tired after firing or being on the range from 10.0am – 4pm.

We have nothing to eat now from breakfast until 5pm as the range is 11/2 hours walk to the camp, so I don't feel inclined to go out at night. The 3/9th H.L.I (Glasgow Highlanders) have just arrived here. They have a fine band. I ought to get into one of the Highland battalions, there are over a dozen now.

There is no more news so I will close with love. Norman.

Editor: *On November 28th 1915 Norman was sent to join 'O' Squad at the School of Instruction at Fulford Barracks in York for a month's musketry training. The day after arriving, 29th November, he was promoted to the rank of Corporal, receiving a grand total of 1/8 per day, approximately £5 in today's money. After completing the course he was given over two weeks' leave, returning to Ripon and duty possibly as late as 9th January 1916. Writing home on the 13th January Norman noted that he was very busy and had had the 'hardest day's work since I enlisted. We attend an officer's and nco's class of*

Swedish Drill [Physical Training] and bayonet fighting every night 5.30pm – 7pm.'

Wed.

Dear Dad

I've just come down to Aunty Edie's for the first time this week as I was doing Swedish Drill on Monday and digging trenches by moonlight last night.

She says that she has heard mentioned that I am going to France in a week or so. Well I was chosen for the draft on Sunday but it will not go this month.

The C.O. is away on his holidays and comes back this week-end. It rests with him who has to go to France and it is certain that he will withdraw me as he has signed my papers for a commission and he also wrote to the Brigadier and asked him to grant me an interview.

The Brigadier sent for me on the 4th but I was on leave. Another interview will be arranged as soon as the C.O. comes back. If I had seen the Brigadier General on the 4th I would have been gazetted this week.

There isn't the least cause for worrying and you needn't mention it to mother. I will write if there is any news.

With best love Norman

Saturday

Dear all

I am sorry I didn't write sooner but I've been busy from 6.30 to 8pm every night this week. We have Swedish Drill 4 nights a week and about 3 lectures.

The C.O. has not rec'd any word from the Brigadier since the 4th of Jan. I am disappointed that I was away on leave then as I would have been gazetted within 10 days.

I've been busy today with a kit inspection

Rising through the ranks: Corporal Norman Collins.

and have also had two men in my room up for orders for staying out until 11pm and sleeping in etc. It isn't all honey looking after a hut with 40 men in, and nearly all 'boozers'. In fact one died yesterday. He drunk himself to death...

We are very short of n.c.o's in our battalion and I am getting plenty of work to do. All this week I have been the senior N.C.O. of the lot. The officer in command (an expeditionary man of 1914) got mixed up and didn't know how to get the men on the parade ground with the front rank in front etc so when we were resting during the march he asked me to tell him what commands to give and I put him right.

Our officers carry packs the same as the men now.

I will write if there is any news during the week.

With love Norman.

L/Sergeant WN Collins
Friday
Dear all
Just a line to let you know of my promotion. I was on orders on Tuesday evening. At present I do not get extra pay but I have the benefit of the Sergeants' Mess. The food is fine and is properly served up by orderlies, cups and saucers etc. Here is a sample of a day's meals.

Breakfast :- sausage, H.P. Sauce, bread, butter and jam with tea in teapots, not out of a bucket.

Dinner :- two or three plates of vegetable soup, roast, stew or pie, H.P. Sauce, pudding with milk and jam.

Tea :- fried fish, H.P., jam etc.

I ought to get fat now.

I am allowed to wear a solid cast metal or silver badge and may get a sergeant's kit. Also I have the privilege of wearing a bayonet out of camp.

No word from the Brigadier yet tho' it will come sometime. I am rather glad that I have risen from private thro' all the stages when I am not 19 until April. I have my meals at the same table as the Regimental Sergt. Major and Coy. Sergt. Majors etc.

The draft went away at 5.30pm today.

Best love Norman

Sat. 12.30pm – just seen the Brigadier General. I was in trousers and very dirty after cleaning the room out. The C.O. took me to him personally and he only asked my age and father's profession then signed them. In about 10 days or 14 look out for L' Sergt. WN Collins to be 2nd lieut. In Seaforth Regt, Rosshire Buffs.

The only notification I will get will be in the *London Gazette*.

Best love N.

Men of the Seaforth Highlanders shortly before their posting to France. Several of these men appear, on closer inspection, to be little more than boys.

Tuesday
15/2/16
Dear all

I have just come off the Main Guard so am not on parade this morning. We have got a new C.O. from the 1st/4th in France, Lieut. Col. David Mason-Macfarlane. He was wounded at Neuve Chapelle when leading the 4th in a charge. [Ed. *Macfarlane was shot through the left thighbone*].

He is very strict and believes in plenty of marching and only turns back when his horse gets tired.

I ought to be gazetted this weekend or early next week. There are no firms in England that make Highland uniforms but they all send to Scotland for them. The Newcastle firms are all very dear. I have price lists from Glasgow, Dundee and London firms and London is easily the best. The majority of our officers go there and the material and prices are very good.

The price of a pair of tartan trousers is £2-5-0. Kilt £5-5-0. The Newcastle firms charge £4-4-0 for a tunic (without badge or buttons). I have a list of all the necessary articles for £40, so will have £10 over.

I will probably be going to Auntie Edie's tonight.

With a bit of luck I shall be home within a fortnight and then the rabbits etc had better look out.

Yours affect. Norman

Another group of Seaforths pose for the camera. The sergeant, second from the right, was killed at Arras in April 1917.

CHAPTER FOUR

The King's Commission

Norman

In April 1916, I was sent off to an officer cadet training college, the 8th Battalion Army Cadet College at Whittington Barracks at Lichfield. There we were demoted from Sergeant to Cadet and were trained by officers and men from Sandhurst, all regular instructors. We were treated rather harshly by these men. I, of course, had become used to a certain amount of prestige as a Sergeant, but a cadet was the lowest form of life in their eyes. We wore no badges of rank, just a white band around our Glengarry to signify the fact that we were trainees, while the instructors seemed to delight in taking it out on anyone who held non-commissioned rank. We were drilled on the barrack square as if we had been in the army for only one day, and this we resented. I certainly did. Any show of discontent was dealt with straightaway, the Instructor who noticed transferred the individual to what was know as the awkward squad and this of course was an insult and hurt very much. All we had to do was to learn to obey orders and smarten up and I think we turned out to be some of the finest drilled cadets in the country.

We studied military law, which was very strict, and learnt about Field Punishment No1. We took musketry and courses in Mills Bombs and Hales Rifle Grenades, the stem of which was pushed down the barrel of a rifle and launched by the use of a blank cartridge.

We learnt everything an officer needed to know from revetting trenches to saluting. At the end of the course some of the men were returned to their regiments and sent to the Somme. I was fortunate and, with a particular friend of mine called James Henderson, was commissioned into the Seaforth Highlanders while Henderson was commissioned into the 8th Argylls.

'C' Coy
Cadet WN Collins
 No 8 Officer Cadet Batt.
Whittington Barr, Lichfield
Monday
Dear all
I have settled down here now and rather like it. The barracks are 3 miles from the village. Reveille is at 6.0am, Parade 7.15-8.0, Breakfast 8.30, Lunch 1.0pm, Tea 4.30pm, Dinner 7.30pm. We have 3 courses for

lunch and for dinner, soup, cheese and biscuits.

There are about 350 here and a lot from the universities, Edinburgh, Glasgow, Oxford, Cambridge, etc. They know nothing at all and drill in civilian clothes or officer's uniform. The instructors are very poor and make a lot of mistakes. We have had turning by numbers and saluting drill today. It is hard lines for Sergeants and Warrant Officers being on the same level as the civilians from the universities. We have half days on Wednesdays and Saturdays as we are not free until after dinner at night on other days.

Will you send me some pyjamas as soon as possible, blue ones, or any nice colours. We were medically examined on Saturday. My stripes are off but I will get the same pay.

There is no more news at present except that there must have been a tremendous storm here last week as all the telegraph poles are down for miles and many broken in two. The snow lies thickly altho' the weather is hot.

Best love Norman.

April 17th 1916
Dear all
Thank you very much for your parcels. The first one was in bad condition. I like the pyjamas very much. The notebook is also useful. I got the soap as well.

In the parcel I got on Sunday, there was the watch, shaving brush, toffee, dates, cigarettes, cake, cheese. We have finished the eatables all but a little bit of cake! Thank you for the cigarettes Dad! And the cake, Mother. Who sent the shaving brush? Who ever it was thank them. Bolton is very kind to send me that fine watch. I will try and get a case for it on Wednesday, I am not going to wear it on parade.

We never get out of barracks here except on Wednesday night, Saturday and Sunday. It is worse than the Fort. We are always scrubbing floors, forming fours etc, doing 160 paces per minute on the square, brushing boots every hour from 5am until 7.30pm when we are free to write up notes until 9.30pm. [We] are called miscellaneous names by Sergeants etc who know nothing, it is a dog's life and several cadets from the firing line want to go back. The NCOs here, Sergeant Majors etc seem to me to be jealous. I don't know how we will live here 4 months. And to think that such silly asses got commissions thrown at them 4 months ago and ex-Sergeants, Warrant Officers have to go through this.

Only 5 men per 100 are allowed a late pass or weekend, and at York every one had a permanent late pass and every weekend. I had a fine weekend in Sheffield a week gone Saturday. Aunty Edie sent my cardigan jacket and a nice pair of socks, Aunty Emma, a book of stamps, Uncle

George 2/6. It is very kind of them.

Everything is done on the double here. We have five minutes to change from the kilt into slacks for physical drill and five minutes after to get into Highland dress, brush our boots and be out on parade again.

On Saturday I was in Tamworth. It is 4½ miles away and has a fine castle. I believe it is mentioned in Scott's works. James VI of Scotland and 1st King of England stayed there and Mary Queen of Scots before she was executed. I was in the Royal bedchamber where there are bloodstains in the oak floor where a murder was committed. The walls are nine feet thick. I was in the dungeons etc. It was very historic. It was raining on Saturday and I was not able to get out until after tea and then had a short walk until dinner. No more news so I will close.

With best love Norman.

PS A boy of 18 from London University has got 14 days in the cells and sent into the army as a private because he refused to sweep underneath an unpaid lance corporal's bed this morning. He is now in the civilian prison at Lichfield. And then they talk about the German bullies. He wasn't told twice to do it and had no warning. Hard luck for a chap who hasn't been under military discipline before.

Monday 17th April
Dear Bolton
I wish I was coming home for good. I was never tired of the army until I became a cadet and the life here is hateful and I would much rather be a sergeant. We are bullied all day long.

Every morning we have to have our beds made up, the room dry-scrubbed, table and forms scrubbed etc before 6am. Then shaved, boots brushed, buttons etc, equipment polished etc and on parade at 6.45. If there is a speck of dirt anywhere we are shouted at, and to go on parade with a pocket button undone is asking for a Court-Martial!

We have a tartar of a Sergeant Major here. He shouts 'Shun, as y' were! Quick march! Halt! Double mark time! About turn, attention!!! all in one sentence. He is about six foot three inches and a tremendous corporation, and a face like a volcano. He reminds me of a gorilla...

I'm going to bed now as I've been working from 5am.

Your loving brother, Norman

Tues 25.4.16
I received your letter on Sunday. 50% of the cadets got leave from Thursday noon until Sunday midnight but as I was at Sheffield for a weekend a fortnight ago I could not get off.

I had a letter from Uncle George today. Ripon Camp is isolated as diphtheria is raging. No soldier is allowed into the town. We are having a better time this week. The summer sports are commencing and we have to go in for cricket, tennis, boxing, running, jumping, swimming etc. I will be sending home for my flannels perhaps in a week or two. It will be fine wearing those grey ones again after being in uniform for a year. I am pleased the weather was fine for the holidays. It would be nice at Hesleden.

Have you settled there for good?

I had a decent time in Tamworth these holidays. We went to the barrack church on Friday and Sunday. Church parade is compulsory in the army you know. I am still a Presbyterian. Whenever we go out to Tamworth we have to motor and it is rather expensive. It is 'infra dig' to go on the bus that passes every two hours and only stops at the barracks if the driver wishes to do so. I am still the only Seaforth here altho' we get new arrivals every week. Every other regiment has about 30 representatives. The Tamworth and Lichfield people seem struck with

P74&75&76&77 Notes made by Norman during officer training at Lichfield.

the brilliant hose tops! The majority of cadets are from France and Egypt. We have a lot of the 14th London Regiment here (London Scottish) and most of them were in that famous charge in October 1914. I have met a lot of chaps who were thro' the Gallipoli Campaign.

Our C.O. was there, and his opinion is that the war will last for at least another two years. That is why these schools were formed, to build up an army of competent officers for the summer and we will probably get the first chance of staying on after the war. If I get a chance I will stick to the army.

We have a lot of Ministers here from Scotland. There are two in my room. There is no more news, so I will close.

With best love
Norman.

74

Aids to Concealment.
aim :- to disturb lie of land as little as possible.
1) Parapet. avoid straight line
2) Short lengths of Firing Line not on same alignment.
3) Bushes in scrubby country
4) Dummy Trenches usually where sods have been cut well from rear.
5) Avoid land lines on hill tops, slope preferable.
- Design -
1) Bullet Proof
2) Inconspicuous
3) Interior slope as steep as possible
4) Wide enough to allow stretcher to pass.

Wednesday 9/5/16

Dear all

We have been on a route march this morning. On Saturday afternoon I was in a Firing Party to fire over the grave of a Gordon who died of wounds last week.

It is a very imposing ceremony. At the grave side we fired three volleys and then presented arms with fixed bayonets while the buglers played 'Last Post'. It rained all the time and we got rather wet.

It is a fine afternoon and I have a lot of studying to do as we have an exam tomorrow on 'Field Engineering' or 'trench digging'.

Do you think the new Military Act will affect you Bolton? Keep out of the army if possible and especially the infantry. [Ed. *conscription was introduced as law in February 1916 as a response to the shortage of manpower in the British Army. For reasons unknown Bolton never did serve in the forces.*]

Every one here thinks there has been a big action in France about February 29-30th [*sic*] on account of the unusual number of officer casualties for that date.

With love

Norman

PS Will you send me my drawing instruments. Compasses, set square etc. Not the ink compasses.

7.00pm Tuesday

Dear Bolton

Thanks for your letter. How did you spend your holidays? Any shooting or football? I may get home for a day or two at Whitsuntide. I will let you know and then you can get my civilian clothes ready.

We have a decent mess here. Easy chairs, games, piano etc. I am growing a 'tasche'. It will be about ready when I am gazetted. I have had ten motor drives since Thursday. Outside work we live exactly the same as officers.

I have given about 3 musketry lectures to the other cadets of my platoon as we are short of instructors. That course at York was very useful.

I have learnt nothing here so far, however I am quite settled down as the longer we are here the longer we will live. I expect I will get out to France about September. I hope the trench warfare is over as it is too monotonous for my taste. All my training has been open warfare. I think Kitchener underestimated the duration when he said 3 years. It won't be much use going back to engineering when I am 21 or more will it? If you ever join, do not join anything but the Inns of Court or Artists Rifles. Even then you would have to be a cadet here. Well I will close now as it is dinner time.

Best love Norman

Tuesday May 16/16

Dear all

Thanks for your letter. I am sending back the watch you sent me as it has never kept going for 12 hours. I had it examined by a first-class jeweller here and he can do nothing with it as it is defective. There is something wrong with the jewels. We expect to get away from here by the end of June as there was an urgent message from the W.O. [*War Office*] about hurrying us through.

I believe there is some heavy fighting going on in France now. The rumour amongst the Expeditionary men here is that the big advance was to begin on May 14th 1916.

The C.O.s are complaining of the lack of officers and there must be a shortage as there have been no second lieutenants gazetted since January and every 50 men enlisted must have an officer. Even the wastages at the Front have not been made up. There are 100 men here who never applied for commissions. The War Office took 1,050 men from one brigade in France to be trained as officers. 500 came from one battalion. That means that there were not a sufficient number applying.

8/5/16 Chapt. III F.E.
Troops that dig trenches should occupy them.
Div. men into reliefs.
Measured by amount work done or length of time.
Task = certain work to do in certain time.
4 hr relief.
Ord. conditions man should dig 80 cu ft. of earth in 4 hours
1st hour = 30
2 " = 25
3 " = 15
4 " = 10
Lifting earth 4' a throw; 12'
Tools Shovel, Pick, spade, crowbar, entrench tool,
100 men. 70 shovels 30 picks.
Length Shovel 3'-1"
Pick -3-0

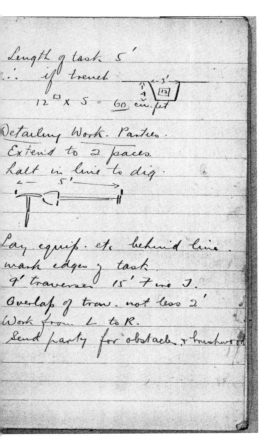

Length of task. 5'
... if trench
$12^{\square} \times 5 = 60$ cu. ft

Detailing Work. Parties.
Extend to 2 paces.
Halt in line to dig.
← 5' →

Lay equip. etc. behind line.
mark edges of task.
9' traverse 15' 7 ins J.
Overlap of trow. not less 2'
Work from L to R.
Send party for obstacle, brushwood

Give my kind regards to all at Hesleden.

Best love Norman

Friday

Did you see the Seaforth casualty list yesterday and also today? I know a lot of them. Some of them have only been out 8 weeks. In one list there were 152 without including killed in officer casualties. Enclosed you will find a weekly exam paper on Topography. They are very easy, A is highest possible.

Saturday July 1st 1916

Dear Bolton

....We all wear officers' uniform now, I believe I told you last week. We are issued with 1 tunic, 2 shirts, 1 tie, caps, breeches, puttees and boots. Highlanders can wear the kilt also. I don't know what use the breeches are. It is a poor idea to deduct £8 from our kit allowance and supply us with badly fitting uniforms from London. My tunic had to go back to the makers 3 times, and the puttees are poor quality. They charge us £2-2s for a pair of boots.

Also men of Highland regiments who were going into English regiments were given cut away tunics and vice-versa causing a lot of dissatisfaction. Men who should have had dyed Glengarry's got black ones. It is a regular mix up. My tunic was 4 f inches small round the chest and 2 inches round the hips and had to have a new front in.

It is harder to get a commission now than in peacetime. About 20% of the cadet battalion have gone or are going back to their units. Three weeks ago we were on parade and a list of names was read out of men to go back. The funny part is that the majority of them have obtained splendid marks in the exams and have good conduct sheets, done well in practical work and yet are told that they are not the class of men wanted. The following are the only 'reasons' given. No personality, too much personality, would probably be too familiar with N.C.O.

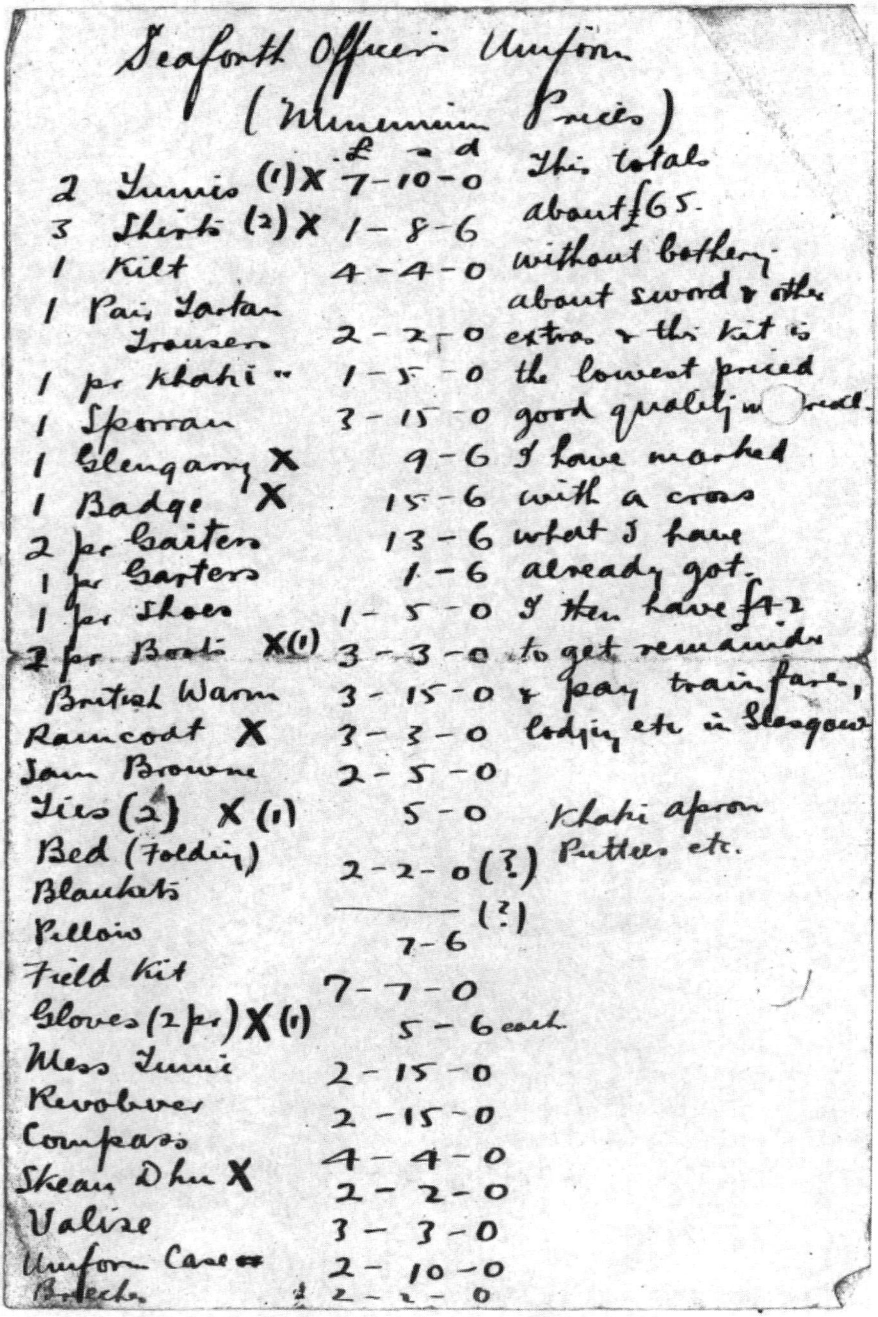

Seaforth Officers Uniform

(Minimum Prices)

	£ - s - d	
2 Tunics (1) X	7 - 10 - 0	This totals
3 Shirts (2) X	1 - 8 - 6	about £65.
1 Kilt	4 - 4 - 0	without bothering
1 Pair Tartan		about sword & other
Trousers	2 - 2 - 0	extras & this kit is
1 pr khaki "	1 - 5 - 0	the lowest priced
1 Sporran	3 - 15 - 0	good quality in real.
1 Glengarry X	9 - 6	I have marked
1 Badge X	15 - 6	with a cross
2 pr Gaiters	13 - 6	what I have
1 pr Garters	1 - 6	already got.
1 pr Shoes	1 - 5 - 0	I then have £2
2 pr Boots X(1)	3 - 3 - 0	to get remainder
British Warm	3 - 15 - 0	& pay train fare,
Raincoat X	3 - 3 - 0	lodging etc in Glasgow
Sam Browne	2 - 5 - 0	
Ties (2) X (1)	5 - 0	Khaki apron
Bed (folding)		Puttees etc.
Blankets	2 - 2 - 0 (?)	
Pillow	——— (?)	
	7 - 6	
Field Kit	7 - 7 - 0	
Gloves (2 pr) X (1)	5 - 6 each	
Mess Tunic	2 - 15 - 0	
Revolver	2 - 15 - 0	
Compass	4 - 4 - 0	
Skean Dhu X	2 - 2 - 0	
Valise	3 - 3 - 0	
Uniform Case	2 - 10 - 0	
Brolly	2 - 2 - 0	

The price of officerdom!

Social position has nothing to do with it, as included in the list are, ministers, graduates of the big universities, M.Sc.s, etc. A number of them are ex-sergeants, who won their chevrons at the front. [Ed. *this is an intriguing dilema. As a response to officer shortages at the front the War Office urgently required an influx of new subalterns. However, those responsible for training were clearly reluctant to compromise pre-war standards.*]

I hope that I have struck the happy medium re. personality. Probably I have been overlooked as I am one of the shortest in the company!

There is a very bad feeling termed 'wind-up' in the battalion, the nervous strain is really awful as no one knows whether he will be the next to go. No one has been gazetted yet, although 'A' Coy has been here four months. I wouldn't go through it again for a dozen commissions. The man who sleeps next to me, Rev R.W.S___ from Glasgow University, two years O.T.C. experience, has been warned [*that he will soon go abroad*]. One has to be worth it before becoming an officer now, and we are not being trained as officers. Many of the men have never been given the chance to drill half a dozen men even. However we go out into the villages round about and are saluted by the men who do not note the absence of the star!

We were told that the recommendations of our C.O.s and Brigadiers do not count if our platoon officer (a sub) does not recommend us for a commission. Yesterday one poor chap who was recommended for a commission in his own battalion in which he had been for six years, went back. Surely if his own C.O. considered him capable after working with him six years, the opinion of a sub-lieutenant shouldn't count especially having known him for only three months.

One of the officers asked me to make him an accurate plan of the trenches we are digging. It is to be hung in the C.O.s Orderly Room. I was congratulated on it. Instructing in musketry has also gone a long way towards helping them to form an opinion of me. Every thing counts here, even appearances, as the disreputable looking ones are being eliminated.

It seems years since I was home. I've never felt the time drag so since I joined the army. By the way I was asking to join the Royal Flying Corps (attached). I would have, but I didn't relish the idea of another course of instruction and also prefer the kilt. The captain tried hard to persuade me. I would have been gazetted straight away.

If the war goes on much longer I won't be much of an engineer when I return as I have forgotten most things I knew. If it isn't finished within a year I will either apply for a cadetship in the Royal Military College and become a regular or go to the navy as an artificer. I could hardly start at the beginning again at the age of 20-21. Excuse this pessimistic letter but it is the general feeling here, in fact when the men are 'oiled' they hunt round for the officers to damage them. I still like the army life but not cadet life when we have no position at all. Best love to Father and Mother. Norman

Editor: *On Friday 7 July Norman was given a weekend pass enabling him to visit his relatives in Sheffield. It was an uncomfortable few days away, as Norman noted again, for as he walked around the town 'Every soldier was saluting me; fine 6 pace salutes! No one seems to notice the absence of the star'. As an officer cadet he was forbidden from returning salutes, leaving him in 'a most embarrassing position'. It was a temporary inconvenience, for throughout July Norman sat his exams, taking any time he could spare to relax by riding in the country near Sutton Coldfield, where he noted how 'people here stare at a kiltie riding a bike'. Fed up with study, where four hour exams were typical, Norman could not wait to finish.*

Tuesday 18/7/16

Dear all

....Our final examination is on Monday and we leave here on the Thursday following. I believe I am going straight to Glasgow for my uniform and then home. I will probably be 10 or 14 days at home before being gazetted. When I am gazetted I will apply to my C.O. for 14 days leave and spend half the time at home and the remainder in Sheffield. We have had a stiff day today and are going out all night leaving barracks at 10pm and returning about 6am tomorrow, so I will have the grass for a bed tonight. This is much better than in trenches where one sees nothing but walls of earth and it's like living in a drain.

Do you think that you could get me some of my clothing as we now only get our Cadet Uniform and £42. The total cost is about £75 so I will only be able to get the essentials at first and save some of my pay to get the others. The Cadet Uniform (£8) was stopped off our government allowance and it is badly made and without collar badges, Regimental buttons or badges of rank. We have to get these on ourselves. Also they made us buy breeches and we are not allowed to wear them in a Highland Regt.

The majority of the men here have money of their own to supplement the Government. I have got my raincoat and Skean Dhu [*the knife that goes down the side of the stocking*] out of my pay and out of the bank. The remainder of the money (about £4-10) I will withdraw this week-end. All I would like you to get would be a few pairs of khaki socks. One pair of Seaforth Garters and one khaki shirt. I enclose a list of kit I will have to get. [Ed. *see page 78*]

I am looking forward to coming home for a holiday, especially in the first week of August. I hope you will get a good holiday, Dad and Bolton. We will have a good time at Hesleden and go down to Blackhalls for a picnic. I don't want mother to do any work when I am home for the holiday week. My salary as a Sub will be about £14 a month.

Ta ta' the noo

Dearest love, Norman

25/7/16

Dear all

The great day is over and our examinations are finished. The final took place yesterday 24th July and now we are waiting for another General to inspect us (probably on Friday) and are then leaving here. The exam lasted about 4 hours and included Military Law, Military Organisation, Topography, Field engineering, interior economy, Infantry training, Trench warfare and musketry, so you see it covered a great deal of ground. Everything connected with it we had learnt in our own time. I have a very high percentage of marks throughout the course, about 80%. This is among the top dozen in the Company at least.

Since writing last I have changed my plans and am coming home first and not getting anything until I am gazetted, unless I am told to do so. I will wear mufti at home. Can you send me a decent leather bag to hold boots, shirts etc not too small.

I will probably send a parcel of things home this week.

I may be home for about 3 weeks. I will telegraph the day I leave which I think will be Saturday. Is Fred Chiverton at home yet? If so give him my kind regards.

I will be glad when I see the last of Lichfield.

Best love Norman

Editor: *Perhaps because Norman was working so hard, perhaps because he was revising for exams, only 12 letters appear to have been written during officer training. Similarly, between receiving his commission and arrival in France there is a curious gap of some two months when letters were either not written or not kept.*

Norman, a newly commissioned second lieutenant.

Norman

On August 16th 1916 I was commissioned at Whittington Barracks into the Seaforth Highlanders, after which I received official notification that I had been 'appointed to a Commission in the 4th (Reserve) Seaforth Highlanders stationed at North Camp, Ripon, Yorks,' being told to 'report to the Adjutant of the above unit at once.' I may have gone to Ripon first, although my memory is that on leaving Lichfield I went to Glasgow to buy my officer's kit. I went with my friend Jock Henderson. We had both gone through the Cadet Battalion at Lichfield together and had been commissioned on the same day, Jock being posted to the Argylls. We did our shopping in Sauchiehall Street having been granted an allowance to buy our officer's kilt, sporran and a claymore – although what we wanted a claymore for in the trenches I do not know. The kilt, however, I came to swear by, for that seven yards of cloth went round your waist and kept it warm. It was wonderful and in my opinion it was the best garment to have in the trenches. Later, when I was in France, and it was wet, I found that it was better to take the kilt off and put it around the shoulders before going into the line. Then, when you got up into the front line you wiped or scooped off all the mud and sweat from your thighs and put your kilt on, tightened it up and you were nice and snug and warm. Trousers and puttees became and stayed wet, it was impossible to get them dry, and trousers were very thin compared to the kilt, there was no comparison. Such insights were, however, learnt from experience, and I was still several weeks away from gaining such knowledge.

With my new uniform I left Scotland and returned to Ripon and waited until I was posted to France. In the meantime we were given refresher courses at the No1 School of Instruction in everything from tactical problem solving to advancing under artillery fire, from lectures on military law to the organisation of bombing parties. I was passing time until, in due course, I would be sent to fill up the vacancies left by those who were killed or had been wounded. Every person who went out as a replacement was fully aware of that. Even so, there was excitement, elation even. I was looking forward to the battle, even though I was a little bit afraid, naturally, not knowing what I was in for, but eager to get there too.

CHAPTER FIVE

Over the Pond

Norman

On October 18th 1916, I left Charing Cross Station to join the regiment in France. I was seen off by Fred Chiverton, my old friend from Hartlepool. He had been the last to see me off when I had changed trains at Newcastle Station, prior to my journey to Scotland and ultimate enlistment at Fort George. Now he was here again, and it was a gesture on his part that I greatly appreciated. He had come down to London especially, so to mark the occasion we popped into a photographer's shop to have our picture taken together.

The Battle of the Somme was in full swing and there had been tremendous casualties.

The Highland regiments were combined into one Division, the 51st Highland Division, which was really reserved for battles. That might sound silly but some regiments did a lot of work in the trenches but did not take part in great battles. The Highland Division was the reverse; it trained for special battles as a rule and they were all Highland, Gordons,

Norman pictured with his good friend Fred Chiverton just hours before the former's embarkation for France.

Black Watch, Seaforths, Camerons, Argylls and so forth, and we all trained together. We trained behind the lines and then, when we were ready, we entered the trenches and were told the Order of Battle.

There was tremendous divisional pride. Oh, for years after the war I wore a gold ring with the Highland Division crest on it, which I had made for me specially. Was I scared? You can't use terms like that. You knew the horrors of war, we knew that 60,000 men had become casualties on July 1st. We went not thinking we'd come out of it, we didn't think we'd live. We hoped we'd live and we hoped we'd get a blighty wound more than anything, a wound that would sent us home.

I was on draft for France and I arrived at the base at Etaples and the Bull Ring where there was a severe form of training; there was no mincing matters there. It was really very cruel indeed for privates and NCOs. In the bayonet fighting, for instance, apart from sticking bayonets into sandbags, there were one or two skulls lying about to illustrate that a bayonet stuck into a bone was difficult to remove. A bayonet was thrust into a skull but could only be removed by sticking your foot on it and shortening your grip on the rifle. There was an object in showing this, of course, but it seemed to me a little bit too much. I have no idea from where these skulls had been acquired.

I was only there a short time before I took a train which meandered slowly eastward for two days to go the sixty miles to the front line. It took an age, not least because the train was pushed constantly into sidings for a time to let more urgent traffic through. I had been commissioned into the 4th Battalion but I was being posted to the 6th because they were well below strength. Almost as soon as I got there, we were told we were going

The Bull Ring at Etaples. Training here was hard and often brutal before the men were sent up the line.

over the top and so we immediately started intensive training behind the line. We were to take the village of Beaumont Hamel. This village had been an objective on 1st July but the attack had failed and so four months later we were to be sent forward to take it. I know we were excited and, by not having been over the top before, were not particularly frightened. The bravest man is very often the one who has not yet seen action.

Editor: *The autumn of 1916 was particularly miserable with wet and cold days punctuated by periods of hard frost and snow. In the line, mud became an almost overwhelming problem as the sides of trenches caved-in owing to inadequate revetments. Dugouts collapsed in several parts of the line near Beaumont Hamel, killing several unsuspecting occupants. It was with some relief that the 6th Battalion Seaforth Highlanders were able to leave the line on Saturday 21st October, proceeding to the village of Forceville, and a hutted encampment. It was from this village that Norman wrote his first letter from the front.*

Oct 23/16
Dear all
...After leaving the base last Friday I was 40 hours in the train before arriving at the firing line. I met the Battalion coming out of the trenches after I had walked about 10 miles. We then marched or rather dragged ourselves to a little village consisting mostly of holes held together by a few bricks.

This is a rest for us. We shovel mud off the roads, drill etc about 1,000 metres from the Bosche. The artillery is well behind us and kick up an awful din, day and night. The sky is one blaze of light from the guns and we can hardly hear one another speak.

We do look guys in our 'tin' helmets. The mud is really awful. Even on the main roads it is up to our boot tops and off the road will drag a man's boots off with puttees on. In the trenches it varies from ankle to almost waist deep and men have to be hauled out sometimes with ropes.

The weather is beastly and we are at present in an open field near a wood. The Bosche shelled the place the other day. The big shells make a noise like a railway train.

For miles behind the line there is a continuous stream of traffic, with only a few inches between each vehicle. One stream goes to and one from the trenches and motor cyclists etc dodge about or rather swim through the mud.

There are some huge guns here and one can hear them at the base.

Water is very scarce for either drinking or washing purposes as we are not allowed to use any but sterilized water. Baths are unknown, I am absolutely filthy with mud and have to scrape it off. On the whole though

The Western Front. In the distance Very lights illuminate No Man's Land.

I prefer this to being at home as I am doing something at last and although it is a very hard life it is not so monotonous.

I am very much in need of cigarettes. Would you send some of those little black nigroids for the throat. You see we sleep in the mud. Cakes and things will be welcome as I am always hungry and any sort of toffee. There is no news and of course, I can't tell it you if there is. I saw a 'tank' yesterday. Some things! Don't forget umpteen parcels of eatables and cigarettes.

You better lodge an order to supply me them, about 100 a week and I will send a cheque.

Best love, Norman

26 Oct 16

Dear All

Just a line to let you know that I am A1.

The only thing to complain about is the mud and cold. It's rained ever since I came out.

I change my socks every day but they are soaked with mud in 10 minutes. We sleep on the wet ones and try and dry them a bit, as we have no fires and the only lights we have are candles and we cannot get those always.

Instead of washing our legs we scrape the mud off with a knife. We have no blankets of course and have to sleep in our wet clothes. Thank goodness I brought the sleeping bag with me. When we are out of the trenches I manage to get a decent sleep. The men have an awful time. They are up to their waists in mud in the trenches and when in billets they sleep on the muddy floors of old barns, stables etc with more hole than roof.

We rarely take any clothes off at all. I always put on everything I have and my pyjamas on top then pile equipment on top of me. Socks will be

In the line. This picture of the 6th Seaforths was taken on the Somme in the spring of 1916 prior to Norman's arrival.

P88&89 *A map of the area on the Somme with which Norman was to become very familiar. The front lines had remained static since the failure of the first assault on the German-held village of Beaumont Hamel on 1st July 1916. Below, the village of Mailly-Maillet through which Norman frequently passed before the second attack on 13th November.*

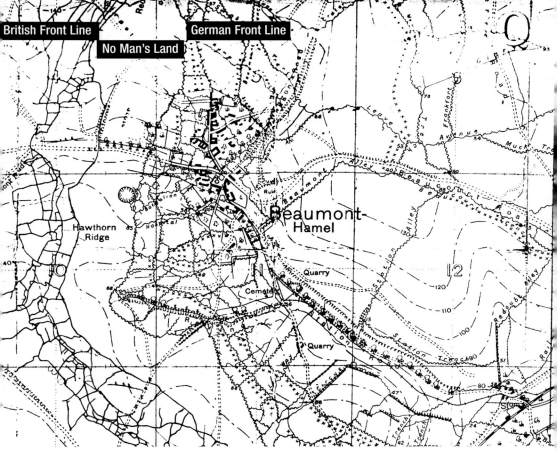

Hawthorn
Ridge

Beaumont-
Hamel

Quarry

Cemetery

Quarry

very welcome and some quinine tablets from Boots for colds. I haven't been more than 48 hours in one place since I came out. At present we are out for a 'rest'. Yesterday I was scraping or rather ladling mud off the road from 8am to 5pm and it rained steadily all day and all this on a sandwich of cheese and bread. This was about a mile from the trenches (firing line) and was our 'rest'. We were well splashed with mud from the traffic. It was funny to see a chap bending down ladling mud with his back to the road and a bus would dash past and he would catch the stream of mud 'where his kilt wasn't'. Excuse this writing but the nearest candle is 2 yards away. I am going to send home to London for a proper trench coat, oiled silk lined as the coats I have simply mop up the wet. Nothing will keep the wet out for long. We do not get a rum ration every day but it is absolutely necessary I think.

We have to censor our men's letters home and it is most amusing sometimes. The average Tommy is quite a cheerful creature though. The Army Service Corps and other non combatant corps are greatly envied out here. They have a decent time. The Royal Garrison Artillery have a soft time. It is a fine sight to see the aeroplanes being shelled. They were doing a lot of that yesterday when I was mud scraping.

Best love Norman

P.S Will you send a Wolseley vest out, long sleeves and any patent comforts you can find.

Norman

We had Hallowe'en before the battle, it was the last day of October, when all the officers gathered together and we had something to eat and there was a lot of heavy drinking and a sing-song. The Pipe Sergeant Major was brought in to play the pipes and they are deafening in a small barn and when he had finished, the Colonel said 'What will you have to drink?' And he said 'I will have a crème de menthe'. And he held out his mug and they filled it up with crème de menthe and he drank it all in one draught. God! I would have thought he was as sick as a dog. I wasn't in a very good condition either because I wasn't a drinker at all, and naturally this was new territory for me. I was thumping the table and there was some broken glass about, and I remember a very kind major restraining me a little bit in case I thumped on the glass, but, worst of all, early that next morning I had to go up the front line with a sergeant to do a reconnaissance before it became light. I got back to billets, a tent it was, and shortly afterwards I set off. I had to catch a lorry, a very primitive lorry, for I can remember the smell of the exhaust was pretty awful, and go up to the line at Beaumont Hamel and do a reconnoitre, over the top, just to have a look round to see what I could see. Well, I was feeling a bit sick, I can tell you, especially with the fumes of the lorry exhaust, when I got up there, in the line. The pair of us went up the communication trench into the front line, up a short ladder and into no man's land and looked. We crawled about there in no man's land but I'm afraid I wasn't really any use because I didn't really know what I was there for, having just got to France and never having been up before. I remember that I froze stiff when a star shell burst. And I had a look round to see what I could see, which wasn't much, and then I had to get back to the regiment because by then it was daybreak, to report to the orderly room to the adjutant.

Nov 3rd 1916

...Thanks very much for the papers, I read every word including adverts about four times. I don't think I've seen a newspaper since leaving the Base. The mud still continues. I never dreamt of such mud. Yesterday I got stuck and couldn't move, I had to be hauled out. My boot came away from the upper and is now being sewn together. Whom do you

Above. The end of a sap or trench from which the cameraman had been afforded a clear sight of the famous basilica in the British-held town of Albert. It is just possible to identify the figure of the Madonna leaning at 120° to the ground as shown in the picture inset. Below, the 6th Seaforths in a trench. The man in the foreground is reading a copy of the popular newspaper The Daily Sketch while the man behind peers through a periscope into No Man's Land.

think I met today? Henderson of the Argylls. I was glad to see him. Bolton met him at Ripon. Yesterday morning at 5am I was in No Man's Land doing a bit of reconnoitoring. You should have seen the 'Strafe' last night. Every gun was turned onto the Bosche and it was one roar all night and the Bosche trenches were one line of fire. They answered it fairly strongly but we have the upper hand on them easily. We rarely see a Bosche aeroplane up. Today I counted ten British observation balloons up and couldn't see an enemy one. Our airmen simply swarm over their trenches. I saw a fine parachute descent from a balloon today.

The thing that strikes me most about the trenches is the small number of men holding the line. One can walk for a hundred yards along the front line trench and never see a soul except a single sentry. We see some rotten sights but it's all in the game... We have umpteen 'tanks' here. I saw thirteen in a row today! They are fearsome things and can climb a slope of 60 degrees or walk through houses.

About nine tenths of the troops out here never see a German. The infantry go through more in one day than the Army Service Corps, Royal Garrison Artillery etc do in six months.

Best love Norman

Sunday 5.11.16

Dear all

The weather is hindering operations out here as per usual. I got a letter, my first from England. It was welcome. Sunday is exactly similar to any other day out here. We often forget which day it is. No rest for the weary! Life out here is quite bearable when one gets used to it. Let me give you a little advice, Bolton. Don't on any account join the infantry if you can possible get into any other branch of the service.

They have double the work of any other branch and are the least thought of. Well there is no more news so au Revoir.

Best Love Norman

P.S I am looking forward to a letter from home. Send some local papers and an occasional *Bystander* and some socks and handkerchiefs.

Tuesday 3pm

7/11/16

Dear Dad and Mother,

I've just finished giving my platoon respirator drill. We are well in the gas zone. Luckily we are out of the trenches at present and resting in a little village behind the trenches. We are in tents, (very leaky).

We are not very much troubled by shell-fire. Occasionally they shove some dirty ones over and sometimes an aeroplane playfully drops a bomb or two. I don't mind it when we're in the trenches but object to it when

The bombing section of A Company, 6th Seaforths, a few weeks prior to their assault on Beaumont Hamel on 13th November.

we want to get a bit of sleep. However, don't worry about me. I'll come through A1.

I've met a lot of chaps out here whom I haven't seen for over a year.

The food is pretty decent. It is nearly all tinned stuff but we've got a gem of a cook who can disguise a cat as a rabbit or turn horseflesh into mutton. We never enquire what the dinner is made of. Every morning (out of the trenches) we get porridge and two eggs! We are only allowed to drink sterilized water and water for ablution purposes is very scarce. However, few people die of under-washing. You ask if I got the flannels. I bought a vest at the Base; that is all. It is now in need of a wash.

Well, I will close now as I have my platoon's letters to censor.

Hope you are quite well

Your loving son, Norman

PS I am posting two letters, one to Hesleden and one to H'pool. Let me know if you get them at different times.

7/11/16

Dear Bolton

Thanks muchly for your welcome letter. It took only five days to come. In one letter I asked for a Wolseley vest, long sleeves and also socks. It is fearfully cold here and I had no time to get a vest at Base. Will you also send me a woollen shirt with collar attached if possible. I will let you have the money when I get back. It is raining as per usual today... I am looking forward to getting the parcel. Hope it is well packed to stand the five days journey. I expect they get roughly treated en route as the men travel in cattle trucks so I don't know what parcels travel in. The brand of cigarettes I like is Army Club, Crayol or any kind almost, preferably Virginia. There is no news here except that last night our slumbers were disturbed by an aeroplane raid.

Ta ta the noo. I will write when your parcel arrives.

Yours to a cinder, Norman

PS Have any of my letters been opened by the base censor?

Nov 9th 1916

Dear Bolton

Rec'd your letter with enclosures last night.

Parcel not yet arrived. It is not overdue yet however as they sometimes take a fortnight to come.

Been cleaning roads today. Going into trenches again tomorrow. Just been giving my feet a good dose of whale oil to prevent frost bite. This is supplied by the Government.

Most interesting today watching our gunners shell Bosche aeroplanes. It is a beautiful sight. The weather was lovely and the sky almost cloudless. The shells usually burst in groups of half-a-dozen and are like stars slowly turning into feathers of smoke. I should think there were about 500 shells fired in half-an-hour.

One was brought down. I hope it will keep fine for a few days, as it is miserable in wet weather.

I have just been having a bottle of champagne with old Henderson of the Argylls. I met him also cleaning roads.

It was like old times. He is also going up the line tomorrow.

...Well I will ring off as I am Orderly Officer and have to be at roll call.

Good night

Yours to a cinder, Norman

PS Best love to Mother and Father. Hope you are all in the pink.

Editor: *Strict censorship would have prevented Norman from giving any indication about the forthcoming attack. Nevertheless, knowing that an attack was imminent, Norman's letters give no impression of nerves or fear; on the contrary, they are upbeat and quite resilient.*

The attack on Beaumont Hamel was part of a wider assault known as The Battle of the Ancre, in which several divisions would attack over a four mile front to take ground which had been stubbornly held by the Germans throughout the Somme offensive. Owing to the weather the attack had been

Going over the top.   IWM Q2104

postponed on several occasions but on Friday 10th operations were re-instituted owing to the relatively fine weather of the previous days, 'Z day' or the day of the attack being fixed for the13th. In the meantime the battalion was kept out of the line so that lectures on discipline could be passed on by company commanders to the NCOs and men. Preparations continued. The following day, Saturday 12th, conferences were held at Battalion Headquarters, during which time precise details of the forthcoming attack were discussed with officers. Elsewhere football matches were played, the Battalion diary noting that D Company beat the Headquarters Company 5 – 0. That evening a concert was given in the Scottish Churches Hut. The next day the Battalion's War Diary noted on Sunday 12th:

'The Battalion rested all day on account of move to trenches at night... At night the men had a good meal, and at 9.20pm the first Company moved off to the trenches. A B and HQ Coys proceeded to Windmill outside Mailly Maillet and C and D Coys went through Mailly Maillet to Auchonvilliers. At these points men were given tea and after a short rest each Company was guided to its position by a guide.'

Owing to the terrible state of the roads and the weight of supplies given to each man to carry, it took all of the six hours allotted to reach the line. Even then the poor state of the communication and assembly trenches ensured the men struggled up to the front, arriving in their allotted positions less than an hour and a half before zero hour at 5.45am. It had been an onerous night although the Battalion diary still felt able to note that all the men were 'in good form and eager.' Norman Collins would lead his men, 6th Platoon, B Company, in the forthcoming assault.

95

Norman

The night before the attack, my batman, a lad called Griger, came to see me and asked if I could provide him with the means of buying a small bottle of whisky – quite illegal of course, but I gave him the money to do it. He would be going over the top with me and he was likely to be killed, as I thought I would be. I thought my chances of coming back were very small, but it doesn't deter you because you have no choice, no alternative. We had been told that we would go over the top in the second wave at six o'clock, so our watches were synchronised and we waited for the creeping barrage that was to cover our advance.

In the hours before the attack I recall speaking with two fellow officers, Lieutenants Smith and Mclean. We'd chatted and joked and I remember Lieutenant Smith telling me one curious thing and that was that he was going to go sick but not until after the attack, if he survived. He had developed a severe rupture and he wanted the hernia attended to in hospital, but he wouldn't go sick beforehand as he had been nominated for the attack and his absence would seem cowardly. I thought that was very brave of him because he could have gone sick and saved his life. In the event he was killed.

As the time to go approaches, you're looking at your watch to see the

An artist's vivid (and inaccurate) idea of how the assault on Beaumont Hamel progressed. The tanks, far from mounting the German front line, became bogged down in No Man's Land. Over the page. The jumping-off trenches for the 51st Division can be clearly seen, as can the damage to the German lines. This picture was taken four days after the advance. One of two ditched tanks is marked 'A' on the photograph.

hour, and then you're looking in front to see when the barrage will open, and then you look and see that your men – the men you're standing to go over the top with – are equipped and ready to go, and that nobody's turned around and gone back.

Everyone went in with fixed bayonets and as many mills bombs as they could carry, except Lewis gunners who carried a revolver and mills bombs. The officers carried a cane, a walking stick, a .45 revolver and they also carried a few bombs. The cane was no use to us whatever, but every officer carried a walking stick, it was just a bit of show. Although I carried a .45 revolver it wasn't until much later, when I went on a shooting course, that I was shown how to use it, because a .45 kicks so heavily that you couldn't hit a barn door at ten yards.

At 6.00am it was still dark and there was a thick fog, then suddenly a mine went up under the enemy line and two thousand guns opened fire and dropped on their trenches. The whole of the horizon seemed to go up in flames. It was so loud you could not pick out individual shells, it was just a continuous drumming. A solid canopy of steel went over our heads.

Then there was dead silence, and the silence was itself stunning; the contrast, and then about two minutes later our artillery raised their sights and dished out their barrage on to their second line. The noise was terrific, although after the main barrage had stopped I could certainly

have spoken to those near to me. I can't recall anything I said, something absolutely ridiculous probably. Even so the men looked to me for encouragement, and you made jokes if you could.

I suppose I might have blown a whistle but it didn't mean anything, so you sort of shepherded the men over. You are very aware of the example you are setting the men; if they saw you funking it – showing fear – they wouldn't think much of you. I went out and saw men dropping right and left; I've a vision of a Gordon Highlander pitching forward with his rifle and bayonet on to his hands and knees. I went up to him and he was stone dead, his kilt raised showing his backside.

You're working in a very small area, the rest of the Front is nothing. You

6TH SEAFORTH Hs

New Beaumont Road

8TH ARGYLE & SUTHERLAND Hs

Sunken Lane

8TH ARGYLE & SUTHERLAND Hs

5TH SEAFORTH Hs

8TH ARGYLE & SUTHERLAND Hs

57E748
57IQ4D
17·11·16 — 2

Ditched Tank

No Man's Land

Crater

German Front Line

Tank Museum No5078/d6

British Front Line

No Man's Land

German Front Line

The morass of Beaumont Hamel. Norman saw almost nothing to suggest a village had ever existed there save for a single washing mangle. IWM Q1546

quickly look to see if a man who had dropped is dead or not or if there was anything you could do for him, but you hadn't time to stop. I had to keep up a certain bearing in front of the men and when you saw men wandering about, which did happen, because to begin with it was dark, and if they had got a bit lost, it was the officer's job to form them into a fighting unit, no matter what regiment they were in. Knowing one's duty took one's mind off the horrible things.

There was a thick mist; then, I remember, when the mist rose and the sun came out, the sun shone on the shell holes full of water and they were all different colours, the chemicals I suppose. My servant went with me, Grigor, and he stuck with me as far as he could all the time. Then you encourage them, right and left, to go with you, all go together and you keep looking as they drop occasionally.

The Germans were taken entirely by surprise and their front line was captured quite easily with few losses. We had cut quite a bit of their defensive wire beforehand and the main German defensive position, known as Y Ravine with its deep dugouts, was taken. I wasn't in the first wave that captured the front line, we advanced through the first waves and went on under a canopy of steel to the second and third lines, where, farther back, the Germans managed to get their machine guns up and they opened fire on our second wave. I must say this, the Germans were good soldiers, many fought to the end. I saw one machine gun nest fight to the last round. I really admired them as soldiers and, if I had to have

a battalion on my right it would be a German battalion and I would never need worry that they would fall back

A small number of men came up on our right from the Naval Division, led by Colonel Freyberg, and entered Beaumont Hamel in front of us at an angle. You couldn't avoid the bullets, or the shells; it was sheer chance. When machine guns are firing, it's like a solid wall of lead. You can smell the gunpowder, well, I suppose nitrates, the high explosives. I was not defenceless, and I fought when the opportunity came. My role was to get into their trenches and throw mills bombs down into the dugouts where the Germans were, I suppose killing quite a number. You throw the bombs down and say 'Share that amongst you'; that's what you said as a rule and all the time I've no doubt whatever that I was as frightened as anything and hoping, a faint hope, that I would survive.

They detached a couple of platoons to clear out the dugouts and we took some hundreds of prisoners. They just said 'Kamarad' and put their hands up before a lance corporal was given the job of taking them out of the line. I remember a young German prisoner coming in, hopping along using a piece of wood as a crutch. I could speak a few words of German and I just asked him how he felt. I had him put on to a stretcher and taken back with our own wounded behind the lines, and I could see that I wasn't very popular at all for that. I was seen as using up a stretcher and a valuable service to help a German at the expense of our own. He was a young fellow and was probably no more than 18; he was badly wounded and he could only hop, and I suppose I felt sorry for him. I couldn't say that German ever got back because I did hear stories of one or two prisoners being killed and in one instance I know one soldier did kill a prisoner, but he had lost two brothers and was a bit demented himself. All I know is that I saw them set off from the trenches to the cages.

There was nothing left of the village of Beaumont Hamel. It had been so badly pulverised by shelling that effectively it could only have been identified by map references. As I walked around I saw in the mud and bricks a washing mangle, two rollers and a cast iron frame and that was practically the only thing left in the village which showed that human beings had ever lived there. A day or two afterwards I had a good look round the German dugouts in Y Ravine. An enormous amount of ammunition and bombs of various descriptions were liberated from the German dugouts. I found one box of German egg grenades, a whole case of them untouched.

The dugouts themselves were very deep and had flights of stairs down to the bottom and wire beds. There was even a system of brass bells, like you would see in a house, which a batman could ring before entry into

Senior German officers await collection and interrogation after their capture during the attack. The legs in the background standing behind the tripod belong to the famous war cinematographer Geoffrey Malins.
IWM Q4503

LIST OF BOOTY CAPTURED IN
BEAUMONT HAMEL ON 13th NOV.

Machine Guns.
Minenwerfers medium.
Minenwerfer Light (2 varieties).
Hotchkiss Gun.
S.A.A. some blunt nosed, and some packets marked KYNOCHS
     FUSIL BELGE: and dummy cartridges.
Bomb store containing:-
    100 boxes S.A.A., each of 320 rounds.
    30 cases of bombs and Grenades.
    56 Iron Kegs about 3 feet high weighing each about
      5 cwts (full) contents unknown.
    7 barrels two thirds of cwt each of black
      explosive powder.
    9 supposed gas cylinders about 8 feet in length.

Bombs.
    Grenades with stick handles (2 kinds).
    Grenades tortoise.
    Bombs Egg.
    Bombs for Minenwerfers.
    Shells with groves cut in copper band and
      cartridge in base, similar to a STOKES bomb.
    Aerial darts.

Flares.
Flare pistols.
Acetylene Gas sets.
Searchlights.
Armourers' shop and tools. including two complete sets of
    tools for medium minenwerfer.

Dry Canteen containing
    Tinned beef. from MONTE VIDEO.
    Norwegian Sardines.
    Cigars.
    Cigarettes, including Will's Goldflake.
    Matches.
    Coffee Beans.
    German "Maconochie" rations.

Piano.
Dancing Slippers.
Soda water.
Women's clothing.
Cat O' Nine Tails.
Lager beer.
Bivouacs.
The incoming Mail.
Rifles long and short.

Some of the booty seized from the German dugouts including 'dancing slippers' and a 'piano'.

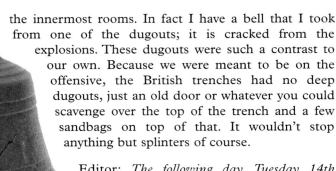

the innermost rooms. In fact I have a bell that I took from one of the dugouts; it is cracked from the explosions. These dugouts were such a contrast to our own. Because we were meant to be on the offensive, the British trenches had no deep dugouts, just an old door or whatever you could scavenge over the top of the trench and a few sandbags on top of that. It wouldn't stop anything but splinters of course.

The bell taken as a souvenir by Norman from a dugout in Y Ravine.

Editor: *The following day, Tuesday 14th November, the Seaforths' War Diary curtly noted that the Battalion was 'holding captured positions but men very scattered'. On the 15th the men were withdrawn to the support lines and awaited relief which duly arrived, allowing the exhausted men to march back to camp at Mailly Maillet, where, as the diary records, the 'men received a hot meal and were made as comfortable as possible. A few men who had been slightly wounded on the 13th rejoined the Battalion'. The next day the Battalion paraded on a hill close to camp where the Roll was called and the Commanding Officer offered his congratulations for the excellent work during the assault. The men spent the remainder of the day cleaning their uniform and kit.*

It is interesting to note that, as an assaulting division, the Highland Division suffered disproportionately during such major engagements. Many units during the war suffered almost as many casualties simply holding the line as they did in attacking the enemy. This is not true for those units held back for assaults in which breaking well-entrenched enemy soldiers would be 'difficult'. A look at the casualty figures shows that during October the four battalions of 152 Brigade, 51st Division, suffered only 44 casualties, of whom just eight were killed. In November, after the attack on Beaumont Hamel, the total casualties were no less than 1,022, of whom at least 285 officers and men were killed. More stark still are the casualty rates suffered by the 6th Seaforth Highlanders. In October the 923 officers and men of the battalion suffered one casualty. In November, of the 587 officers and men who took part in the attack at Beaumont Hamel, some 277 were killed, wounded or missing, including 14 officers. The Battalion diary notes that 'Those who went over the parapet in the actual assault suffered 45% losses,' optimistically adding that 'It will be seen, however, that the total losses suffered by the Brigade did not exceed the number of prisoners captured;' – some comfort to the men of the Battalion, perhaps. As a young Second Lieutenant new to the rigours of trench warfare, Norman had been very lucky to come out unscathed.

The Battalion diary records the fate of those officers who were less fortunate:

'Monday 20th

Battalion in reserve in line near dugouts in Seaforth Trench. Salvage of tools bombs etc. Bodies of those killed on 13th being brought in. Bodies of Captain EJ Anderson, 2Lt RA Mclean, RJ Smith taken down to cemetery at Mailly Maillet.

'Tuesday 21st

Salvage work continues. Captain EJ Anderson, 2/Lts RA Mclean and RJ Smith buried this morning in Mailly Maillet Cemetery at 9.am Captain AH Macgregor's body recovered this morning and taken to cemetery at Mailly Maillet.'

Norman

I remember writing a little poem later, when I was in hospital, in memory of my two friends Lieutenants Smith and Mclean, killed in the attack

Right. Pte Percy Dickin of A Company, 6th Seaforths, who was killed in the attack. Pte Dickin kept a diary during his service in France in 1916 and handed it to his platoon sergeant for safe-keeping during the fighting. The last entry, written on 12th November, simply states 'preparations for attack'. In the event, Pte Dickin's body was lost and his name is now commemorated on the Thiepval Memorial to the missing of the Somme. Below, dead Highlanders left on the battlefield. IWM Q11657

and who now lie side by side. I still have this little poem which is just doggerel, it is not poetry at all, but it expresses my feelings at the time.

In Memoriam Lieutenants RJ Smith and RA McLean, killed at Beaumont Hamel the 13 November 1916.

When this blessed war is over
And the roar of the guns shall cease
We shall soon get tried of working
And the monotony of peace.
We shall think of the days behind us
Of the barrage's devilish roar
Of the machine guns' steady rattle
And dream we are back once more
No more in the cold wet trenches
Where the ghoulish rats abound
Where we cursed like hell when the minnies fell
And the shrapnel burst around.
No more over the top we'll go
Lashed by a storm of shell
As we charged, with a curse
Through bullets and worse
And laughed on the brink of hell.
And when in a bed we lay dying
We'll think of our dead comrades' graves
Where the spirits of before surround them
And the ghost of a barrage still waves.
Twas there in the crashing barrage
Two comrades of mine went west
They played a straight game and played it well
But now they are forever at rest.
We laughed and swore together
In the trenches on the Somme
And jested with fate and fought like men
And wondered when death would come.
But now they are gone forever
As if they had never been born
But they are dead and happy
But their mothers are left to mourn.
We laid them at Mailly, side by side
In sound of the British guns
They had won their earth by right of their birth
For they will bring us sons.
Then down in our dugout whey and worn
We rested from the fight

I wrote to our mothers and sweethearts at home
By the guttering candle's light.
But I hope against hope
When the last post sounds
And the judgement day is at hand
That the soldiers who died and the soldiers who lived
Will meet in the promised land.

After the attack I was appointed burial officer and was told just to get on with the job of burying the dead. I had a squad of men to help me, carrying picks and shovels, and also stretchers. Of course some of the men they were picking up were their brothers and cousins and they of course were very upset, very very upset. Their number included my two particular friends Smith and Mclean; both had been killed in the action. Lt Smith had been a dentist in civilian life, and Lt Mclean a divinity student; it shows you the waste of life there was in that war.

In a Highland Regiment, there were many men from the same family, village or town. I mean some of them obviously were just crying, and it was quite natural. If your brother was picked up on a battlefield like that, well, you've only got to imagine what you would feel like, and that's exactly what they felt like.

We took the dead on stretchers back to Mailly Maillet Wood and dug a long trench and put the dead in there, wrapped in an army blanket, neatly packed in like sardines. They fell side by side and they were buried side by side. We covered them up and we gave them a proper funeral with reversed arms: all the ceremonial of a proper funeral, blowing the Last Post and the pipes playing 'Flowers in the Forest'. I think there were about 80; it might have been less. And Smith and McClean; I saw them buried there too. As an officer you needn't stand aloof, but the best way of comforting the living would be to give them a stroke on the head or a pat on the back or some gesture like that, without words. But it was a horrible thing to do, to have to bury your own cousin or brother.

I thought we were finished, but afterwards I was told to go back into what had been no man's land and bury the old dead of the Newfoundland Regiment, killed on 1st July. I was given three platoons which carried picks and shovels and, still under shell fire, we buried them in shell holes.

The flesh had gone mainly from the face but the hair had still grown, the beard to some extent. When bodies have lain out for a long time there is a sweet smell, and it is not as repulsive as one might suppose. I thought 'there but for the grace of God go I', but the sight didn't make me any

A picture of British dead taken by a German photographer. Above, the cemetery at Mailly-Maillet. The dead Seaforths who were buried here were afforded greater care by Norman. However, the close proximity of their bodies during burial has ensured that the gravestones above ground are somewhat compacted.

386

braver when I had to go into my next attack.

The dead Newfoundlanders looked very ragged, and the rats were running out of their chests. The rats were getting out of the rain, of course, because the cloth over the rib cage made quite a nice nest and I should think this was the driest place they could find in no man's land. However, when you touched a body the rats just poured out of the front. A dozen bodies would be touched simultaneously and there were rats tumbling everywhere. To think that a human being provided a nest for a rat was a pretty dreadful feeling. The puttees on the men's legs looked quite round but when the flesh goes from under the puttee, there is just a bone, and if you stand on it, it just squashes. For a young fellow like myself, nineteen, all I had to look forward to at the time was a similar fate. It still has an effect on me now; you never forget it. After the war I used to have nightmares and heavy dreams, dreams of all kinds. For years I was back there on the Somme.

I remember the mine crater at Beaumont Hamel, which was blown on July 1st and blown again for our attack. It was close to where I was burying the Newfoundlanders, so for a short while I wondered over and walked down into the crater. However, it was very loose and you could see all sorts of things that were lying about, jackboots, and I decided it was better to get out because the soil was slipping away and I could easily have been buried.

Nobody knew what to do, we were all fresh, all newcomers to the job. All we could do was remove the paybooks. These were in quite good condition as they were in a sort of oil cloth which protected them. Photographs of mothers and fathers and sweethearts and children were all in the pay books, and of course their last will and testament. I don't know how many we collected – hundreds I suppose. We left their identity disc on so they could be identified later, and put the personal items in a clean sandbag. Then we shovelled the dead into shell holes, most half-filled with water, about thirty rotting bodies to a shell hole, and covered them up as best we could. We tried where we could to get a bit of wood and make a mark to identify the place. In the setting sun I saw once again the green and blue tinge to the shell water, and it looked rather beautiful.

There was no emotion then. There comes a time when emotion becomes a strange sort of word, you get so much that you become deadened to it, you're bound to. You didn't know men that had been dead for four and a half months and were strangers to you, you only knew them as young soldiers and officers who'd gone to war just as you had, and they'd died. You felt in a way horrified to think that there you had, in my case, probably nine hundred or so young men – they must have been an average age of nineteen or twenty, who had all come over to France to do what they thought no doubt would be a wonderful job of work and in

The cemetery at Mailly-Maillet just after the war, and today.

one day – one day – they were destroyed. You thought then, and you saw what happened, and you realised what their aspirations and their ambitions were and what they were going to do to put the world right, and they were going to do this and that, and all they did was to die in really a few minutes. Yet you couldn't weep for them any more than you could for any of the other 20,000 who died on 1 July, but it seemed to me to be such a terrible waste of life.

Editor: *The Brigade diary notes in simple detail the onerous work undertaken by nineteen year old Norman and the men under his command. On November*

111

The crater blown under the German lines on 1st July was reblown on 13th November. It is pictured shortly after the successful attack. The crater's sides were dangerous and liable to slippage.

20th is records that:

'Large parties were employed in collecting the dead and loading the bodies on to wagons, nearly 100 bodies being collected', while the following day a further '144 bodies were recovered.' On November 22nd the diary notes that in total '630 British bodies of men killed on 1 July and 8 Germans have been buried, and a further 90 bodies have been collected of men killed on November 13th and transported to Auchonvilliers Cemetery. The area is now clear of dead except for a few Germans.' On the 24th the diary recorded:

'During this period of duty in the trenches the battlefield was almost entirely cleared, not only were all the bodies of those killed on Nov 13th collected and transported to Auchonvilliers cemetery but 669 skeletons which were found lying out in "No Man's Land" were buried. These were the remains of soldiers of the 2nd Seaforth Highrs, Middlesex Regt, Royal Fusiliers and a Newfoundland Inf. Regt who had been killed on July 1st; on the battle front of one of our battalions about 545 of these skeletons were buried. Few identifications of them could be obtained as their identity discs had either been removed previously or had been eaten by rats which swarmed amongst the corpses. Altogether the bodies of a little short of 1,000 soldiers were dealt with.'

Norman

Finally, this loathsome job was finished and with one or two men I took the sandbags full of pay books down a communication trench to Brigade Headquarters. I noticed as we went that the communication trenches had bodies, and parts of bodies, sticking out of the wall for quite a long way. The trench, I suppose, had been dug through the bodies where they lay. Occasionally you would see a loose head or two kicking about.

At Brigade headquarters I handed the sandbags over. I was in a deep dugout in the chalk, and I stood there amazed by the luxury of the officers who were down there. I was asked very politely to have a cup of tea, and they handed me some cakes, which I ate. It was incredible. I was glad then to get up. I couldn't really face it. I was feeling a bit under the weather but in front of me I noticed some parcels and I saw that these lovely cakes came from a box labelled 'Fortnum and Mason, Piccadilly'.

It did seem strange that a short distance away you had the war going on and heavy shelling and in this dugout you were back in London, so that even at the front there were stark differences between those in and those close to the line. By this time in the war, many junior officers were wearing other ranks' uniforms. In English regiments many officers had taken to wearing puttees and other ranks' tunics. In Scottish regiments, the kilt was the same for everyone; however when we were in the line we wore an other rank's tunic. So many officers had been picked off while wearing a Sam Browne belt, which no doubt shone with the efforts of the batman that morning. So we all wore a tommy's jacket in the line and the only badge of rank was pencilled in indelible pencil on the shoulder strap, one triangle for a 2nd Lieutenant, two for a Lieutenant, three for a Captain. But the officers down this dugout all had red tabs on and they were all spick and span, polished boots and Sam Browne belts. And there I was dirty, and probably lousy, wearing just a tommy's uniform. I've never forgotten that and I rather resented it. I was very pleased to get out and get back to my men, up the communication trench with my little crew and back into the trenches. I was more at

Norman wearing his officer's tunic and Sam Browne belt. These clearly identified the wearer as a British officer and they were often discarded in action as they attracted German sniper fire.

home with them. I didn't like the idea of leaving the survivors of my own men – they depended on me for things that other people couldn't give them.

It was the closest bond because we were both living in the same world. It's extraordinary really, because the association between officers and men as a rule was very short. Neither lived very long, but during that period it became the most intense feeling. Your affection for the men under you – there's no doubt about that. We used to write to their mothers when they were killed, and the mothers used to reply asking for some sort of memento, 'Have you any little thing you could send us to remind us of our dear boy?', which you could never send, of course. It was really quite pathetic. I don't believe we ever replied to these letters, otherwise we would have been entering into correspondence and I believe there was an order forbidding this.

It took us all our time to write these letters. They always gave these jobs to young 2nd Lieutenants, and the letters I'm afraid had little variation amongst them because when you had to write these letters, sometimes there were about sixty to pen, and you didn't even know who you were talking about. We always tried to write a nice letter to the mother or father because we felt for them, we understood what they were feeling. 'Dear Mr and Mrs So and So, I'm sorry to have to tell you that, as you no doubt have already heard by telegram, your dear son was killed on such a such a date. He was a fine chap and I was very fond of him and he was a good soldier and you, I'm sure, are very proud of him' and so on and so forth. As much as you could do, you made her feel that her son was a hero and that's about all. There was quite a bit of hype, there's no disguising it. There must have been hypocrisy in it, but it was kindly hypocrisy, you were doing it to comfort the mother. By the time you got to the stage of writing fifty or sixty letters, you couldn't remember who they were – too many. But at the time when they were killed you certainly felt for them very much, very much.

Beaumont Hamel
25/11/16
Dear all

It is with great thankfulness that I have so far come through the Battle of the Ancre without a scratch.

The last fortnight has been absolute hell. On the 13th at dawn the Battalion went over the 'bags' [Ed. *sandbags, in other words over the top*] and after a few hours hard fighting captured four lines of trench and the village en route, that the Boche has held for over two years.

It was a magnificent success and our division has made a name for itself.

114

Letters sent to Norman by the bereaved after they had received confirmation of a loved one's death.

On July 1st the Regulars attempted the feat and failed. I suppose you will know all about it from the papers.

We were relieved on the Wednesday following and, after two days rest to be reorganised, went in the trenches again in support.

This morning we came out again much to my relief.

I have had my first wash and shave for a week!

I needed it badly.

There are only 2 officers of my company left now and I am one of them.

For 3 days I have been O.C. party collecting the dead and it was the most loathsome job I've ever had.

We were shelled heavily all the time as of course we were working in the open in full view of the Boche. He used to spot us from his observation balloons and aeroplanes and send over 'crumps' [*5.9″ shells*] and shrapnel.

I had a few of my party knocked out and had some miraculous escapes.

A 6″ [*shell*] on one occasion burst 10 yards away but I was only covered with mud.

We are back a few miles for a short rest. Yesterday I had tea with the Brigadier General as he was so pleased with the work done.

His dugout was a splendid place.

I have a few souvenirs but I don't know whether I'll get them home. I had a helmet but left it as it was too big to carry. However, I still have a fine Boche officer's automatic pistol, a bayonet, some bells from the door of a Boche dug-out, shoulder straps etc. I could have got dozens of things but was too busy, and the one I most value is myself.

My word, you should have seen and heard the barrage. Every minute four shells burst on every yard of the ground.

The [*German*] trenches were just wiped out and it was only by the mouth of the dugouts that one could tell that there had been a trench.

I expect that we will get a rest soon, for a month, at any rate we will not be going over the 'bags' again for some time so don't worry. By the way Henderson had a narrow squeak. He was hit by a piece of shell that went through his belt, tunic, and buckle on his kilt knocking him over for a few minutes! He brought his company out of action alone. He's a splendid fellow and wishes to be remembered to you.

Well, there is no more news, so ta! ta!

Best love, Norman

P.S. My poor servant was 'nah-poohed' and I haven't found the body.

[Ed. *nah-poohed, soldier's slang for finished, ended or, in this case, dead. Derived from the French 'il n' y en a plus', literally meaning 'There is no more'.*]

28/11/16

Dear Mother and all

I am keeping quite well and am not in the trenches again yet. We have moved into an old house and are quite comfortable. This is the first time I've had a roof over me for 6 weeks. You will have received a letter written after the big battle I should think. I've had enough of 'pushes' for a long time. Just had a letter from Sheffield. I hope you are all well. They say that Bolton is going to Sheffield for Xmas. I am sure he will have a jolly time. I wouldn't mind popping in for the day. I certainly hope I'm not in the trenches then.

Been busy writing to the different homes in Elgin and Glasgow etc of the 'B' Coy men knocked out... I found my old servant (Grigor). I'm very

sorry about him as he did look after me well. I wrote home to his mother. He has a brother in this battalion also.

I was reading a paper on the 'push' and it gave the Naval Division a lot of credit for work we did.

Best love
Norman

Editor: *Norman's reference to writing to Grigor's mother is interesting. As already noted, Norman was responsible for writing to the families of all those killed in his platoon, a routine job that would nevertheless have been emotionally trying, regardless of how uniform the letters inevitably became. In three cases, at least, Norman received replies, heart-breaking letters which he chose to keep all his long life.*

Mrs Phin
479 Gairbarid St
Maryhill, Glasgow
Dec 4th 1916
Dear Mr Collins

I now write to thank you for your kind letter of sympathy you so kindly sent to me on my sore Bereavement. It is too cruel to think my darling boy is gone for ever, I do miss his letters so much for he wrote to me regular and never grumbled. But it was a great comfort to me to hear from you and to speak so highly of him and I know very well that it is for a good cause we are fighting. But only if his sweet young life had only been spared I cannot realise he is gone and that I will never see him again.

Well dear Sir I hope and pray that you may get through all right and that your nearest and dearest may be spared the terrible blow that the sad news brings for it just breaks a mothers heart it's the worst I ever got whatever I hope you will over look the liberty I have taken in writing to you but I felt I must thank you.

With all good wishes for your safety I remain
Yours truly
M Phin

Easterton
By Fochabers
1916 Dec 5
Dear Sir

With deep regret I have received your note informing me of the death of my son William witch you say fell on the 13th of Nov under the circumstance it is a great blow to me you have recovered his body which I am glad to hear and buried in a cemerity behind the lines. I have no word yet up till now from the War Office but I suppose it will come through time.

Sir I would ask you if there is any little thing belonging to my son you can find I would be very pleased to get I thank you very much for sending me notice of my sons Death it was very kind of you.

George Mckenzie Yours truly

671 Hawthorn St
Springburn, Glasgow
4th Dec 1916
Dear Sir

On behalf of myself and family I have to thank you for your letter of condolence to us in our sad Bereavement. Arthur was the youngest member of our family, and we feel his loss the more on that account. He was intensely proud of being a Scot, and proud of his Mackenzie tartan kilt. He spent the major part of his life here with us at Home, but you, his officer would see him passing from boyhood into manhood in those 4 months he was under your care in France.

We would be ever grateful to you if you could give us a little more information about the lad regarding how he died. Also if it is at all possible that we may have some little remembrance of him such as his Pocket Book or anything of a like nature we would cherish and prize it above all things.

If it is not in your power to do such, perhaps some of the lads who were his companions in France would oblige us.

Again thanking you for your kindness to us in our Hour of Sorrow

I remain

Yours sincerely

Geo Henry

Editor: *Arthur was just eighteen when he was killed. In all certainty he enlisted aged seventeen and should not have been sent to France, nineteen being the age for service overseas in the British Army. From the letter above it is clear that he was there with the tacit approval of his parents.*

29/11

Dear Bolton

Your letter of the 18th inst. just arrived tonight (11 days). Did I tell you I had received the shirt? Thanks muchly.

It's very cold here today, but we are having a decent time. Fritz put over a few 'coalboxes' [*5.9″ shells*] as I was having breakfast this morning. We will probably have an easy time for a few days after our Beaumont Hamel touch [*attack*].

Today we had saluting drill. Isn't that the British army all over?

The winter pie has also arrived. Thank you very much. A *Bystander* or *Tatler* would be welcome in fact anything readable.

Do you know what we found in Boche Dug-outs? Wills Gold Flake cigs and Scotch Whisky! Also South American tinned meats. Where on earth do they get it? There were some cat-o-nine tails, piano etc. [Ed. *see page 103*]

I haven't seen Henderson since my last spell in the trenches. Kind regards to the picnic crowd.

Well, I'll ring off now. Good night. Schlafen Sie Wohl.

Yours to a cinder,

Norman

Two officers rest in a shell hole in somewhat dryer conditions.

A 6th Seaforth looks towards the German lines. The fact that he is so exposed underlines the fact that he must be some distance from the enemy.

30/11

Dear all

No luck today for me, as there was no letter (our chief joy in life out here). Only 25 days to Christmas and then my leave won't be far away. I will spend 2 days in Sheffield and about 6 at home. We get 10 days from leaving France. It was just 6 weeks yesterday since I landed in France and it is like 6 months. Some people are lucky enough to get that long at the Base. That other parcel of eatables that you sent off on the 18th is about due now. They usually take about 10 days although the one with the shirt in beat your letter of the same date.

Have you had any more word about you being called up, Bolton? Well, take my advice and don't worry about getting out here. You know how keen I was about the army and wanting to get out here, so I know what I'm talking about.

It is the nearest approach to Hell on earth that there is.

I was speaking to a regular who was through Mons, Marne, Aisne, Beaumont Hamel (July 1st) and he said the fighting then was a picnic compared to what it is now.

All the same I prefer to be doing my bit out here than slacking at Ripon. Someone has to do it. The Army Service Corps and Royal Garrison Artillery etc have a decent time. The former are hard worked but they don't see the horrors of war.

Best love Norman

1/12/16 4.0pm

Dear Mother and Father

Weather still cold. Had a quiet time today. Was testing gas helmets this morning. The 'tear' gas is funny stuff. The least whiff in the air makes one's eyes water so that one cannot see. It smells exactly like pear drops and has the same effect as a spoonful of mustard taken internally.

Had no letters today.

Your affectionate son, Norman

1/12/16 7pm

Dear Bolton

Two parcels just arrived, one 18/11/16 and the other 24/11/16. Thanks very much they were very welcome. The cakes are a bit hard but the other things A1. Please do not send any tinned stuff (fruit etc) as we can get those here also those bread cakes soon get hard. The sweet cakes are all right, chocolate, cigs etc. If you could pack them in wooden chocolate boxes they would be fresher I think. I like the dates very much. They were a pleasant surprise. Aunty Louisa sent a fine fleece lined waistcoat. I needed it! She also sent socks, butterscotch and cigarettes.

I could do with a thick pair of khaki hose-tops. I have a fine pair of boots that I bought from the Ordnance. They are Field Boots and come to the top of my hose-tops. It is so wet however in the trenches that the water soaks through after a few hours and also gets in over the top when it is knee deep.

I expect to be into the trenches any time now. They will be the old Boche 'trenches' or rather the remains of them after our artillery practised on them. I expect we will be engaged all night repairing them. There is one comfort however. We will have decent dugouts although of course the entrance will be facing the wrong way. This means a shell from the Boche guns can go right down into the dugout. We are as safe as houses in them as nothing less than an 8inch can do them much damage.

Last time I was in the trenches my dugout got about a dozen direct hits by 6inch shells and didn't hurt anyone. The Boche had spotted it, and so about 50 yards of trench between Headquarters and my dug-out was absolutely unpassable so whenever anyone walked to get there they had to go overland (we were in support). The second night Fritz began putting 'crumps' over and every night after that for a week. We got about 12 a day on to it or near it.

Best love Norman

Dec 2 1916

Dear Mother and Dad

Your letter was very welcome. I am keeping quite well and rather busy.

I think I have got all your parcels. They are always very welcome. You should have received my letter written on the 25th Nov. by now and several later ones. We moved about a fortnight ago. In January we expect to get a rest for a month or two, as the Division has been at the Front since March 1916, without a rest, and some Divisions get a rest every few months. That will be fine as you will have no cause to worry when I am out of the danger-zone.

I will let you know how I spend Xmas and New Year and also as soon as we get our rest. I will write again this week.

Your loving son

Norman.

CHAPTER SIX

Hell! Here Comes a Whizz-Bang

Editor: *Norman's anticipation of an easier time after the exertions of November, belied the fact that the 4th Seaforth Highlanders were still expected to occupy the front line trenches as part of the normal trench routine. On 8th December a draft of 112 other ranks joined the battalion, while church services were held for all denominations prior to their being ordered back up the line the following day. In the meantime the majority of the men waited and rested as far as possible.*

Norman

We had been withdrawn to Auchonvilliers for a rest where we soon got back into our officers' togs. However, whilst we were out of the line, I was detailed, probably because I was the youngest officer, to go back up the line with a working party. I thought this most unfair because we had just come out of action. This working party had to march to a dump and pick up barbed wire and posts and take them up a communication trench. We

A working party on the Somme heading for the frontline.

were to do some re-vetting in a trench and then we were to get out, after dark, in front of the line and mend the wire.

We were on a metalled road just before we entered the communication trench. We had just passed a first aid station on the left, tiny little thing, and as we were going forward I heard a shriek, and I knew a lot about the shriek of shells by this time and I thought 'My God this one's got my name on it'. I recognised it as a coalbox, a 5.9 inch shell. The screech got louder and louder, it was going to drop very near me. My body tensed up as the shell burst on the metalled road just behind me. I pitched forward. The shell must have passed over my shoulder almost. As the smoke cleared I saw that most of my men had been either killed or wounded. I felt all right at first but I put my hand down to my leg and found it covered in blood. Splinters of shell had been driven into my thigh at the back. I looked around, then with the help of one or two men who were sheltering nearby I began to get the wounded into this little first aid post.

There was a young doctor in there and, poor chap, he was shaking like a leaf. He looked at the men and said one by one, 'Dead, dead, put them to one side'. When a man is killed he turns a sort of clay colour, straight away, with the shock, the doctor knew straight away that they were dead. I was a bit numb but, anyway, after a while, an ambulance came up the road and the doctor said 'Now get the wounded all in the ambulance,'

An ambulance makes its way back gingerly over a rickety bridge.

and then said, 'You had better get in too.' These chaps of mine, they were badly wounded and they were crying and screaming because of the bumping of the ambulance. I remember the light guns, and then further back the heavy artillery firing on each side of the road. I lay on my side all the way as we drove until we got to a large marquee, a proper first aid post. There I sat for a little while until the more seriously wounded were attended to, then I was seen and the task began to probe for pieces of shell embedded in my leg. Well, they had rather a difficult time because they were putting a kind of lancet with a hook on the end and were hooking small pieces of shell out. I remember the doctor putting each bit in an ashtray and saying, jokingly, 'There we are, now you can have those set in a ring for your girlfriend'.

Editor: *'An incident on the Albert-Bapaume Road', as Norman came to call the shell explosion that so nearly wiped out his working party, was turned into verse, many years later.*

Norman
    'Twas on the road to Pozières
    One grey December day
    A road that's shelled to blazes
    On which machine guns play.

    A score of stalwart Kilties
    With an officer at their head,
    Marched up that road to Pozieres
    With slow and steady tread.

    It may have been an atom,
    In Fate's gigantic hand,
    But it was the last march of many
    In that gallant little band.

    Their fate is drawing nearer
    Their last journey nearly o'er,
    For a 'Coalbox' comes with a hellish shriek,
    And bursts with a thundering roar.

    Half of that gallant twenty
    Escaped the steely rain;
    The rest have answered the Roll Call,
    And will never march again.

Editor: *In all the confusion it seems likely that Norman may have*

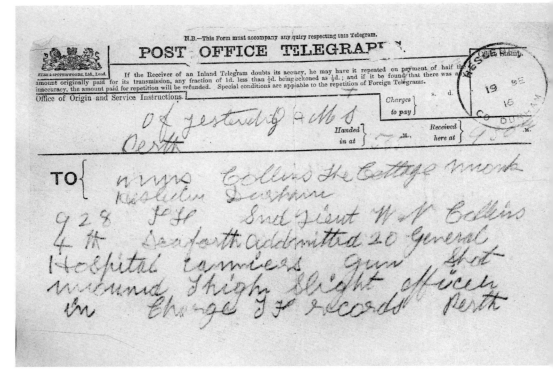

N.B.—This Form must accompany any quiry respecting this Telegram.

POST OFFICE TELEGRAPH

The official telegram to his parents that Norman had been wounded.

overestimated the number of casualties to his 'little band'. Nevertheless the Battalion diary makes no mention of the incident on 8th December other than to remark 'Casualties 3 OR wounded'. One of these men, Private Samuel Cull, was in fact killed, while another, Private George Douglas, died the next day of his injuries. It is a little curious that no reference is made to the wounding of an officer, who is normally named in person. Official notification of Norman's wound came by way of two telegrams dated 14 and 19 December. The later is reproduced above, the former set out below.

Post Office Telegram
'To: Collins, 7 Rowell St, Hartlepool. Regret to inform you 2/Lieut W N Collins fourth Seaforths wounded December 8th. No particulars given, further information will be wired immediately received.'

Editor: *After being picked up by an ambulance Norman was sent on a gruelling seventeen mile journey to the 29th Casualty Clearing Station, which was based at Gézaincourt, near Doullens, a major BEF Base. He arrived on 9th December, one of 55 men admitted that day.*

128

Dec 10th 1916
29th CCS, France
Dear All

I'm getting on A1 and enjoying the rest. It is a great change to being up the line, and what a relief to be clear of shell fire for a few days!

I am a 'walking case' as the wound is just a flesh one. This is better than having to lie in bed.

The nurses are jolly decent. There is no news at all so I will close. My letters from England will go to the battalion and then I don't know where. The 6th is in the trenches at present. They will know that I am wounded but won't know where I am, as I was brought here by ambulance motor from the place I was wounded. Well ta ta

Best love, Norman xx

11th Dec 1916
Dear all

Last night another chap came in to Hospital from the 6th Seaforths. I think his nerves have given way. He always was windy if there were a few shells near.

The weather seems to be improving although at present I don't mind what it is like. Don't send any parcels here as I will probably be moving soon. It will soon be Christmas now. Hope you will enjoy yourselves.

I'll probably be back in the trenches by then, altho' I hope not.

There is no more news.

Henderson of the Argylls was all right when I saw him last week. I will write to him and let him know I'm wounded.

Ta! ta! With best love, Norman.

12th December
Dear all

It is snowing heavily today and I am a lot better off here than in the trenches with the Battalion.

At present they are occupying shell-holes joined together and can only get to them at night as the ground is too sticky to dig communication trenches. The Division is just ready to collapse, having been in the line since February without a rest. We were promised a rest after the show on the 13th November but it is still only a promise.

The nurses are very kind. I hear that leave is stopped for some time. It is a shame that there are people out here who haven't been to Blighty for 18 months and never missed a turn in the trenches. It's wonderful how they stick it.

No more news
With best love, Norman.

13th Dec

Dear Bolton

I've just heard that one of our Lieutenants [JW Blair] has been taken prisoner. You see, as we are just holding shell holes, it is hard to distinguish ours from the Bosches', in the dark.

I am getting along splendidly, though I think I will always carry a piece of shell about with me as a 'souvenir' as it has gone in fairly deeply and the Doc doesn't want to rake about for it.

I slipped out for a walk today, against orders of course, but I wasn't missed. Soon be Christmas now eh! Have a good time. Love to the mater and pater.

Your loving brother Norman

P.S Will be able to swank with a gold braid when I'm at home! The chaps wear them out here but I think it's silly. [Ed. *Norman is referring to a Wound Stripe introduced in July 1916, a two inch long strip of brass worn on the left sleeve of the tunic to denote a wound suffered in action.*]

Editor: *Second Lieutenant JW Blair and a sergeant had in fact been captured while passing from one post to another in No Man's Land, where they were surprised to bump into a German patrol. A single shot was heard, and a number of raised voices; then silence. Both men returned from Germany at the end of the war.*

Owing to the fact that the Somme Battle was over, the number of casualties that arrived at the CCS had lessened considerably and Norman, instead of being moved on down the line quickly, stayed for several days until transferred by Ambulance Train to the 20th General Hospital at Camiers, close to the coast and just to the north of Etaples. Norman was to stay in hospital for just under two weeks before being sent to England. His injury was noted at the time as 'Gun shot wound thigh slight'.

20th General Hospital

(Camiers) France

Dear all

I am now in a Base hospital and getting on A1. I have been here four days. On Wednesday or Thursday, I was operated on and had some shell removed and have been a bit seedy until today.

I haven't been allowed to get up yet and haven't had anything to eat for a week. I will make up for this at Christmas or new year!.

The journey from the 29th CCS was a bit trying as I could only lie on one side and was 9 hours in the train.

I expected to be in Blighty for Christmas and so did the nurses here, but the doctor thinks otherwise.

Your letters will come in less than two days now so I expect a reply for

Christmas. Don't send any cigs at present as I cannot smoke.

On a clear day one can see England from here. So near and yet so far!

Well, Merry Christmas

With best love Norman

Editor: *Within days of arriving at the Base Hospital, Norman was on his way home. Soldiers often hoped for a Blighty wound, one serious enough to instigate a return to England, but not serious enough to impair future long-term prospects. Norman's injury, although considered 'slight', was serious enough to effect a transfer across the Channel where, on landing, he was taken to Brighton and to a workhouse that had been converted into a hospital by the Australians. 'There was a song at the time, "Christmas day in the workhouse" recalled Norman later, 'and I was literally there!'*

Kitchener's Hospital 'H' Block, Brighton, Dec 22nd/16 7pm

Dear All

I Left the Base at 5am 21st and arrived at Calais about 12 noon the same day. We were put on board the boat (the *Brighton*) but did not sail until 7 in the morning (22nd). It was very rough crossing and I was about the only one in the ward that wasn't sick, but I did feel bad!

The people in this hospital are all Australian (God's own people as they say).

Wounded soldiers are carried from an ambulance train to waiting hospital ships at Calais.

You will have received my telegram from Dover. I sent it from the Hospital train. I do not expect to be long here. It is time I was getting up. I am still on milk diet and am getting anxious for Christmas! I will get about three weeks leave after this... All my kit is at the Front near Courcelette (nr Pozières) and I will not get it for months probably. All I have is what I was wearing when I was hit.

I haven't a hat at all as I left my steel helmet at the Casualty Clearing Station and my hose-tapes were lost somewhere. My helmet had a big dent in it where it stopped a piece of stone. (At the time I hardly felt the crump). I see that the name of the officer of our lot who was captured by the Bosche the day after I was hit, is in the casualty list today. The C.O. here says I will be on full rations for Christmas so that will be A1.

With best love Norman

Dec 23rd
Dear All
I got up today for the first time and I was jolly glad. I've been sitting beside the fire all day reading and having occasional '40 winks'. With a bit of luck I should be home in a week. I had a high fever with the wound in France so I had to stay in bed. It was funny being bundled about on a stretcher all the way from the Front (we are all ticketed to say who and what we are etc and this is tied onto our pyjamas).

Hope you have a merry Christmas wherever you are.
With dearest love, Norman

Editor: *Norman's positive attitude no doubt calmed any fears that his parents might have had, although in reality he was not as 'chipper' as he wished to make out. Years later, he recalled that he was 'in bed and pretty sick too. I was very feverish. The nurses tried to get me on my feet for a Christmas party, but I'm afraid I was too far gone for that, but what they did, these dear Australian nurses, they pushed a bottle of whisky under the bed for me to help myself if I felt like it, but of course I couldn't think of touching whisky and I just listened to the festivities going on amongst the patients and the nurses.' His recovery was swift, nevertheless.*

Dec 26th Brighton
Dear Father and Mother
I hope you had a jolly time yesterday. I was allowed to go down to the Dining Room and tuck in at the turkey and plum duff. It's the first Xmas dinner I've eaten in pyjamas and a dressing gown. In the afternoon I went to bed and had a sleep. I may be allowed out tomorrow or the next day as I can walk alright now.

Best wishes for a happy new year. Your loving son Norman

Norman

Within a week or so, I was much improved, to the extent that I thought I would take a trip to London, although I wasn't really fit for it. I didn't ask anybody's permission and I went and caught the Southern Belle, the special train from Brighton to London. I had a walk around and felt a bit better. Later, I went to a music hall and even managed to pop into a restaurant for a snack. Despite the rationing, it was possible to eat as much as you liked in the restaurants; they didn't seem to be short of anything from memory, and the population knew very little about the war. I made my way back to hospital where I got an old-fashioned scolding from the nurses for taking the liberty of walking out.

Editor: As Norman recovered, he continued to write home, although his letters contain little of interest at this time. He noted that his kit, left near Pozières on the day of his injury, had duly arrived, 'almost complete', including his revolver. He also notes that he received several 'shoulder epaulets of departed Fritz's and Karl's' which he forwarded to home. His slightly glib comment, as a nineteen year old, masked the fact that for the rest of his life these were highly personal artefacts.

Such was the speed of Norman's recovery that by 17th January he had already received word from the War Office that a Medical Board was being assembled at Ripon. On the 24th, the Board pronounced Norman fit for General Service, after which his Commanding Officer granted him leave. He returned to Ripon in early February for a week's course of physical training and then musketry while he waited to be placed on a draft for France. Norman's enthusiasm for war was, understandably, waning: in a letter in February, he writes anxiously that 'A new War Office order states that no fit men from France are to be kept in England more than four weeks',

Norman recuperating in England. Note the heavy strapping on his left leg.

133

Norman lighting a cigarette with two off-duty nurses, proudly displaying his wound strip on his left forearm.

A Vest Pocket Camera (VPK) similar to that bought by Norman in March 1917 and with which he took his first snaps some of which are shown.

Captain Harris (centre) before his departure to France to join the 4th Battalion Seaforth Highlanders in 1915. He later became Norman's company officer.

adding, 'I do not know if this applies to officers.'

In the end, Norman remained with the reserve battalion at Ripon for three months. His apparent return to full health hid the fact that inside his body undetected shell casing remained. In due course an abscess began to form at the top of his thigh, which grew and grew before, as Norman noted, 'finally out popped another piece of shell and also a piece of kilt which had been rotting away inside my leg. I discovered that the shell fragments had scraped the main artery, a doctor telling me afterwards that if they had been closer by the thickness of a cigarette paper, I would have bled to death.' The medical problems necessitated a further operation, 'opening up the left side of my abdomen and removing a number of veins and debris that I had collected.' An undated and hastily written note to his parents followed the operation's success.

'I didn't want to tell you I was going through an operation as I thought you might worry about nothing,' he assured them. 'I will be out of bed and able to walk in a few more days.'

Norman

Apart from my operation, my stay at Ripon was uneventful. I waited to return to France along with other officers, some who had been convalescent, others who were awaiting their first time up the line. I met quite a number including one, Otto Murray Dixon, a Lieutenant and artist who I think was related to the Duchess of Sutherland. I shared quarters with him and I got to know him very well. He was a charming man, not a very efficient soldier, and could never remember to step off with the left foot on parade.

Otto was a good artist and I remember watching him draw as we sat in a Nissan hut. He got a jam jar and put some clover in it and drew a rabbit peeping out of the top; he called it 'In clover' and it appeared on the front page of The London Sporting and Dramatic Magazine. Later, in France, he did a sketch of a rat eating food out of a machonochie tin, and that also appeared in the magazine.

Another officer with whom I became friendly was a man called AA Pitcairn and he was a London solicitor and he was the oldest officer in the battalion; I think he was almost old enough to be my father. But I admired him for his pluck for joining the PBI when he could so easily have avoided it altogether. I don't think he ever went over the top but he didn't shirk anything either.

Pitcairn, I was lucky to meet on many a long weekend after the war; Otto, sadly not. He was a very brave officer and led his men over the top on the opening day of the Battle of Arras. As he attacked, he had his belly blown out and he died a day or two later. I went to his grave about seventy years later at Arras. Now, I had only known him a very short time, probably not more than three weeks or a month, but I knew him so well – because in that war you never got to know people for very long, but if

'A hunting we shall go' A group of recuperating officers with trusted shotguns.

you did get to know anyone you got to know them intensely.

In mid March I purchased a little Vest Pocket Kodak camera (VPK) and proceeded to photograph several of those waiting to go back to France. The weather was good and I took many pictures of my brother officers who were later killed, Balantyne, Robson among them. In a letter home, I enthusiastically wrote, 'Yesterday I got my first lot of photos. They are splendid. I will keep a print of every one I take in an album. They will be very interesting after the war.' Owning a camera at the front was against all regulations, so I carried it in a pocket in my khaki apron worn over my kilt. Nobody ever suspected that I had it and, in time, I took pictures of my troops before and after the Battle of Arras and shortly before 3rd Ypres. It was difficult to get film so I had to be very sparing. Even so I very quickly ran out.

I bought the camera partly because I knew that, this time, I would be sent to my own battalion, the 4th Battalion, and would therefore be an officer amongst the men with whom I had enlisted. I think I certainly found it much more homely to be with people I knew.

AA Pitcairn, a friend and fellow officer, who accompanied Norman back to France in April 1917.

CHAPTER SEVEN

Back in the Frying Pan

Editor: *On 9 April, the 4th Seaforth Highlanders took part in the successful attack on Vimy Ridge. The storming of one of the Western Front's few heights has gone down in history as primarily a Canadian action. However, the 51st Division played an integral part. Attacking at 4.45am, the Battalion took all its objectives, managing to link up with the Canadians on their left. In the process, the Battalion captured 167 prisoners, seizing two German machine guns and six trench mortars. The attack cost the Seaforth Highlanders dear. Five officers were killed, including Norman's friend Otto Murray Dixon, and four wounded, while 210 other ranks were killed or wounded and seven were missing. The rash of casualties ensured that, by the end of the month, Norman would be on a draft back to France.*

A group of soldiers pause for breath shortly after a successful action at Arras.

4th (Res) Seaforth Highlanders
North Camp, Ripon
18/4/17
Dear all

Thanks very much for your nice presents, needless to say the Grey's chocolate etc have joined their forefathers.

The weather is very bad today. As I expected it was the Highland Division that took Vimy Ridge. We have had letters from the colonels of the 4th and 6th Battalions and they say that the Canadians on our left had a much easier time and yet there wasn't one word in the papers about our crowd.

The 6th had 400 casualties out of 420 in one day and every officer killed or wounded. This means that the 4th 5th and 6th must have lost at least 1,000 men and 30 officers and we have to supply them. At the most I don't think we could raise 400.

Yesterday I applied for my Draft Leave so I may be home before this letter.

With best love Norman

Editor: *The losses had to be made up by a new draft of men and so it was that Norman was among ten officers who travelled to France two weeks later. These officers would be badly needed, for the day before the draft's departure the Battalion took part in a second attack, on the 23rd April, around the village of Roeux. More casualties were sustained; indeed of the thirty-one officers serving in the Battalion at the start of the month, only fourteen remained at the front. In total, the 4th Seaforths had lost 368 men killed, wounded and missing, about 40% of its fighting strength.*

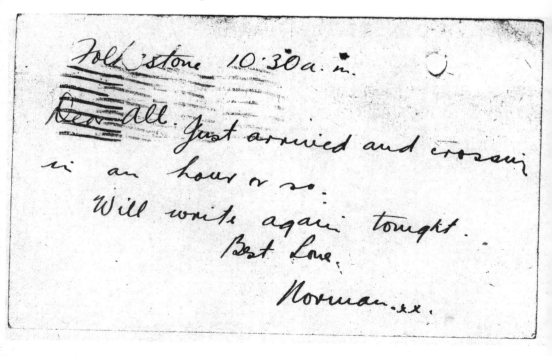

Folkestone 10.30a.m.

Dear all. Just arrived and crossing in an hour or so. Will write again tonight. Best Love, Norman. xx.

Above, a first sight of France, second time around. Below, having just landed, Norman snaps his friends including Pitcairn on the right.

Going up the line to 'find' the battalion.

Editor: *Norman joined the Battalion on the 29th April at the village of Maisières, where he began taking photographs almost immediately. The Battalion diary notes that on the 29th, ten officers arrived: Second Lieutenants G Robson, J Davidson, WN Collins, WS Dane, A Brodie, JN Macdonald, J Bain, M Murray, DBM Jackson and RC Spence. Of these, Norman Collins and Davidson were sent to B Company, along with two other friends from Ripon, AA Pitcairn and Ballantyne, both of whom arrived at the Battalion on the 3rd May.*

Monday
29th April
Dear All
I am at present staying at a farm. Not like Bairnsfather's but quite a good one.

The Division is recuperating after its hard work.

As usual the Battalion has covered itself with glory.

The 7th Argyll and Sutherland Highlanders as you would see in the papers also distinguished itself. I believe one of ours is getting the VC. [Ed. *Lieutenant Donald MacKintosh, 2nd Seaforth Highlanders, was awarded the VC posthumously*]

The weather is beautiful at present. I have met a lot of boys I knew at Fort George in 1915. My Platoon Sergeant enlisted the same day as I did at Dingwall. I won't be in the line for a few days at least. You need not send much out. About the only things we need are cigarettes and toffee and such things as preserved dates.

We left about half of our draft at the base.

There is no more news and I have to get on parade.

Best love

Norman xxx

2/5/17

Dear all

How are you keeping?

I am in the 'Pink' as usual. Today I am orderly officer whose only duties are to inspect the Guard and the billets.

We are having a very quiet time at present and having splendid weather. Tonight we are having a bit of a concert. Of course we are the artistes. Someone has unearthed an old piano. More or less in tune.

The Divisional General [*Harper*] is coming to hear our band.

We have a fine pipe band (sporrans, spats and dyed hose tops)

I will write again tomorrow

Best Love

Norman

6/5/17

Dear Bolton

...We are having it very hot, it's like July or August.

Give my love to all the wee lassies, the little darlings.

Old Pitcairn (another little drink) is with me in my Company. It was lucky that we should get to the same battalion.

Just had tea with JD Pollock VC. Cameron Highlanders. He is a top hole chap.

I had a letter returned to me that I wrote to Henderson of the Argylls when he was in France. He must have been wounded before receiving my letter. The letter was sent back from France to Ripon and then back to France!

The fighting is terrific at present. There is no trench warfare. It is all

Men of the 4th Seaforths practising musketry.

going over the top, one Division after another, until we break through. Fritz is putting up a great fight.

Our Division was in action on the 9th and 23rd and will be ready for another turn in a few days I expect. As usual I will come through all right.

There is no more news so ta ta

Best love to mother and father.

Norman

Editor: *While out of the line at Maisières relations with local people could often become strained; indeed, one unfortunate incident might have marred relations straight away. The diary for 154 Brigade describes extensive training 7 May, as 'not very successful'. The Seaforth Highlanders had used live ammunition and, as the diary noted, had forgotten 'to clear the countryside with the result that they nearly killed several civilians and their horses who were working in the fields. Naturally the General Officer Commanding was somewhat annoyed. However, they were stopped before any damage was done.'*

The Seaforths remained at Maisières until 12 May; they then marched to Etrun on the Arras-St Pol road, where they were housed in huts for two days until sudden orders arrived sending the Seaforths up the line.

16th May 1917
Dear all
Just a note to let you know I am 'all correct' so far.
We are in the line at present and of course enjoying it.
Going to get on the move in a few minutes.
Au Revoir
With best love
Norman xxx

Editor: *There was good reason for the brevity of Norman's note home. During the night there had been a bombardment, several large calibre shells falling near the Seaforths' billets. At 8am that morning, it was reported that the enemy had attacked and were holding the Chemical Works near Rouex. The Chemical Works had been the scene of so much bitter fighting over the previous weeks, finally falling to the 4th Division. News that the Germans had reoccupied the Works was a serious development, so the 4th Seaforth Highlanders were ordered to move up at once to the Arras-Lens Railway embankment, north of the River Scarpe, to await further orders.*

At 2pm, B and D Company were led forward to relieve the 8th Argyll and Sutherland Highlanders in the front line. The Germans were shelling the trenches heavily and it wasn't until early evening that the Seaforths reached the support line known as Corona Trench. Believing that in all likelihood the front line was now held by the Germans, the men were led forward in an attack. Just as the order was to be given to charge, Scottish voices were heard, averting at the last moment a full scale assault on their own positions.

The Chemical Works at Roeux before the Arras offensive.

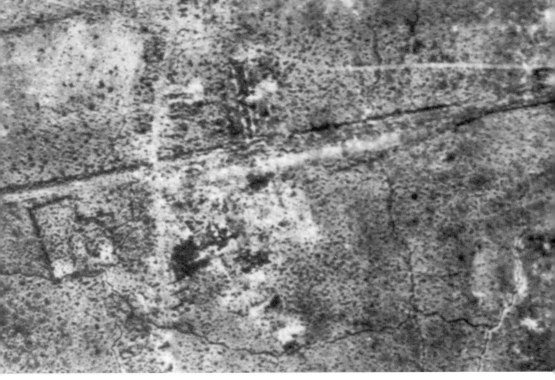

The same ground after the April attack with the Chemical Works almost obliterated.

May 22nd 1917

Dear all

I am quite all right. This open warfare is very funny though.

We received instructions to capture a certain trench last Wednesday night [16th May]. The artillery put up a barrage and we went over partly through little bits of trench and partly over the top. When we got there we found that the trench was already held by our own men.

The Boche put up three lines of 'crump' barrage and I had about the worst hour going through that, that I've ever had. I was partly buried and very slightly wounded. One piece in the hand and one in the leg.

We held the line for 5 days and have just come out. The Germans were on our right and left flanks as it was a very advanced position. One night they assembled for a counter-attack. Our artillery smashed them up. There are hundreds of dead lying about. The trenches are blocked with them in many places and the stench is terrible. There are scores of wounded Boche lying about. We got some collected who had been lying out wounded for 10 days.

Goodness knows how they lived. Of course most of them were too far gone.

I found some of ours as well who had lain out for 4 or 5 days.
There is no more news. We are in reserve at present in the open.
Love Norman xx

Norman

Shelling was constant as we made our way towards the front line. I know I was blown off my feet by a small shell on one occasion. The explosion also caught my bearer, Simpson, who landed on top of me.

When we entered the trench it had been extremely battered. I remember having to climb out of the communication trench to let the troops who had been fighting pass by while we lay on top. The weather had been bad, as I remember, and at several places arms and bottoms of corpses were sticking out of the communication trench. In the support trench the men had tried to repair the line too, and, as the mud had begun to dry out, so bits and pieces were sticking out of the wall. A feature of Roeux was the Chemical Works and another was the cemetery. This had been blown to pieces and a lot of graves churned up, which was a terrible sight. There were dead all over the place, both Germans and our own men, from the attacks and counter attacks that had been going on for over a month.

Of the attack itself, it was something of an abortive affair, and in the end the fighting we expected didn't materialise. We didn't know that then of course, and, as we waited to go, our chances of living, we felt, were cut down to minutes and seconds. It was dark and the shelling was merciless, although their impact was greatly reduced by the soft ground. It meant, however, that all over the battlefield at Roeux there were dud shells; the place was simply littered with them, and bits of equipment, and dying men.

We went over the top and advanced, quietly at first, using

A remarkable image of a 5.9 inch German shell exploding close to Norman.

147

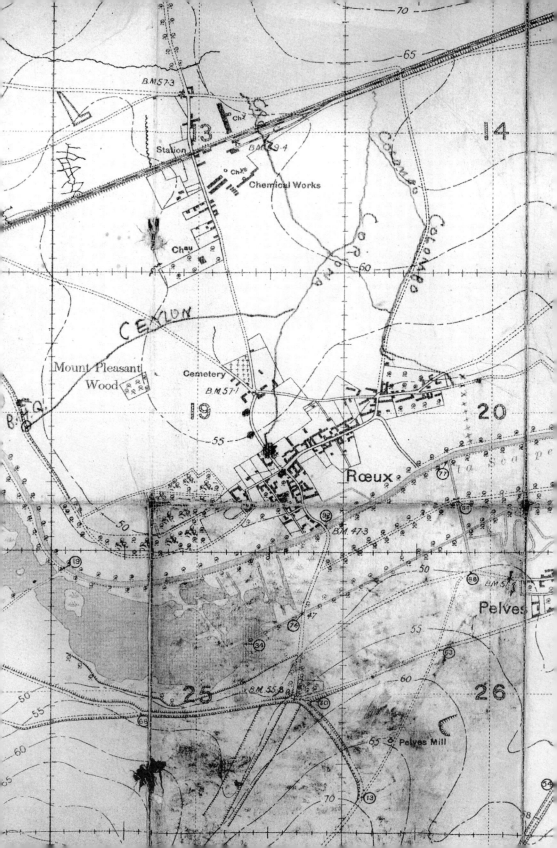

the dark to conceal our presence, and that is all I recall, except for one thing. As we went forward I remember Captain [*Claude Hamilton*] Jack Harris waving for me to come on, and I ran forward and flopped on the ground beside him. We were still being heavily shelled at the time and I did a very silly thing. I took my tin helmet and I rolled it, like Charlie Chaplin used to do with his bowler hat, and put it back on again. That's the way I reported to Captain Harris, with a little joke like that.

We dug in shortly afterwards, taking over from the Argylls, and my friend Jock Henderson, of course, although I didn't see him. We were in the support trench, Corona Trench, and much work had to be done to try and create some semblance of order as the line had been almost obliterated. There was an overwhelming stench of death here. I saw many wounded men, and you never got them in, you couldn't get them in, and they might have their intestines blown out. You could lose most of your guts and still live, dying gradually. It was terrible hearing the wounded out in no man's land at night, crying out in pain, and it affected us very much. We did try and go out at night to bring them in, but many were too badly wounded to help, and it was better just to give them a dose of morphine. They died often talking about their families or their childhoods.

Editor: *Amongst the dead and injured close to the British line was one German body on which Norman found the following, moving letter. It is now preserved amongst Norman's papers held at the Imperial War Museum. Today, historians maintain that, while casualties were terrible for all sides during the previous year's fighting on the Somme, the rate of attrition was, for the Germans, unsustainable.*

The following letter seems to bear out the plight in which the German Army had found itself in early 1917. The original wording seems to indicate that the writer of the letter was an elderly gentleman.

Cassel 14.1.1917
My dear friend
I have received your letter. While the content of your [*letters*] has always given me great pleasure in the past, your latest one has put me into rather a sad mood. Above all, this comes from your telling me that the harshness of life during the time you have spent on the Somme has made such a strong impact on you that you have wished for death. I am truly sorry to hear this. I know you to be a person who is content with a modest lot in life, and I can appreciate how hard things must have been to bring you to such thoughts. Fortune is certainly inflicting a tough time on our dear comrades, who have to achieve, and suffer, tremendous things out there. But then again I know from my dear friend Kloppmann that, in his case,

A trench map carried by Norman during the fighting around Roeux in May 1917. The shaded area is original dirt from the battlefield.

these moods can quickly be driven away if there is someone around who puts himself in his position and recognizes the superhuman achievement for what it is. And, my dear friend, you know that our commander-in-chief is aware of the value of what you are doing and has spoken so often and so enthusiastically about the heroic courage and the heroic temperament of his fighters, and in this way has shown the Fatherland what it owes to its defenders; and from my heart I hope that our dear Germany will always be eager to show its gratitude to its sons. If it can cheer you up a little, accept my assurance that I value you greatly and that I am firmly convinced that you always and fully do your duty. I do hope that you have now been given the opportunity to recover from the strains of recent weeks. That's what I wish for you with my whole heart, and even more I desire that it may soon be granted to us to obtain peace. Even though it is being said everywhere and all the time that peace is still unthinkable, yet I cannot but believe that the thought of peace, now that it has been conveyed to the world by our Kaiser, will become unstoppable. I've been an optimist all my life, and have had no bad experiences because of it, and intend to remain one. I also ran into your brother a few times, when he was on leave over Christmas. I suppose he is now already back in the middle of things. I have had a letter from Goldhahn in Bucharest, and recently one too from Schlau. Yes, I'm now very satisfied with my second tenor, and very proud of him. Well, what a joy it will be when we are all together once more. Gögel writes frequently too. You are, all four of you, to have a letter from me today. I've started with yours, because it weighed heaviest on my heart. So for now I wish you all the best from my heart, and equally from my heart I send you my greetings.

Yours Flörcke, who hopes soon to have another sign of life from you.

Editor: *The identity of the recipient, who had so earnestly wished for death, remains a mystery. It is not known if Norman understood the exact contents of the letter. However, he was moved enough by what he discovered that his intention at the time was to post the letter back to the sender after the war. Another curiosity concerns the circumstances in which Norman found the above letter. In his possessions there is a metal identity disc to a German soldier named Kloppmann, surely the soldier referred to in the letter above. Was Kloppmann killed before the recipient of the letter, or the other way around? Either way it seems inconceivable that these items were not taken from one body.*

Norman

Bombardments were terrible for both sides. We felt we had more in common with the German infantry sitting perhaps one hundred yards away than we did with our own or their gunners, who never seemed to shoot at each other but were always intent on bombarding us. This was especially true with our heavy artillery which was situated, in some cases, miles behind the line. We were under the same conditions as the Germans: they were in muddy trenches; they were suffering under intensive shellfire. It was rather like a big boxer hitting a little man who was undefended. We didn't feel any real animosity towards them.

At night, when I used to go out on patrol into no man's land, we crawled very often from shell hole to shell hole, with saps connecting them, and got very close to the German wire and we could hear them

TAKEN FROM FRANCE. 1917
GERMAN. W.N. Collins
CAPT. SEAFORTH HIGHLANDERS

Cassel, den 14. 1. 1917.

Mein lieber Kamerad!

Jhren lieben Brief habe ich erhalten. Wenn ich sonst immer über den Jnhalt derselben mich so recht von herzen gefreut habe, so hat der letzte Jhrer Briefe mich etwas traurig gestim Vor allem die Mitteilung, dass des Lebens Härte in der Zeit Jhres Aufenthaltes an der Somme Jhnen so stark entgegenge- treten ist, dass Sie sich den Tod gewünscht haben. Das tut mir wirklich sehr leid. Joh kenne Sie als einen Menschen, der mit einem bescheidenen Schicksal zu frieden ist und weiss es zu wü würdigen, wie schwer es gewesen sein muss, wenn Sie auf einen solchen Gedanken gekommen sind. Ja, das Schicksal spielt hart mit unseren lieben Kameraden, die da draussen unmenschliches leisten und über sich ergehen lassen müssen. Dann aber wieder weiss ich von meinem lieben Kamerad Kloppmann, dass diese

talking. On more than one occasion we called out to them; indeed a few of our chaps threw tins of bully beef over and they reciprocated by throwing some German cigars to us. We felt pretty sure we were dealing with people we could make friends with, and a lot of them spoke English.

This fraternization happened on at least one occasion in the line at Rouex before we attacked, and then of course the harmony was disturbed for quite a time afterwards.

German soldiers try to rebuild their trench after a direct hit from British artillery.

After such intense fighting you always had men lying out in No Man's Land, probably with their testicles blown off and crying in agony and lying out there all night long in the dark, in the rain. Most would never have survived. But you had a choice. They could die in agony or you could shoot them. You were shown how to do the thing very cleanly. You would take your .45 revolver and talk to the man and kneel behind him and whilst you were talking pull the trigger, put a bullet through the back of his head and immediately the whole of the front skull came away and they were dead instantly. There was no pain about it, but I can honestly say this, that I never had the courage – because that's what it took – I never had the courage myself to shoot a wounded soldier. I carried out the operation many times afterwards on animals. I could kill a pet dog far better than a vet could, but I was never able to shoot a wounded soldier. I probably should have. My friend, Otto Murray Dixon, was wounded in the stomach in the Arras attack in April. He was in great agony from what I was told. The kindest thing would have been to shoot him on the battlefield. Instead of that, they took him back to hospital and he died days later. It's a tremendous thing to shoot a friend, even though he's in agony, and I just didn't have the courage to do it. Most of them died overnight but of course they didn't thank you for it, I'm sure.

During daylight we took what rest we could, although on several occasions we were attacked by German aircraft, which, toward the end of the day would dive low, perhaps a couple of hundred feet or less, and strafe our trenches before returning to base. On one occasion, a plane flew very, very low and we all fired and I actually emptied my .45 revolver at him although of course I didn't hit anything. People laugh at this, but early one morning, a plane was brought crashing to the ground by Lewis Gun fire from our trench. Other planes were simply driven off by machine gun fire, including several red-coloured aircraft that, I believe, were part of the famous Flying Circus.

Among my possessions from that time in the line is a mud-covered map, on which are marked in little dots the places where I sited the Lewis Guns at one end of Corona trench, in what was left of Roeux. [Ed. *see page 148*] In charge of one of the guns was a lance corporal of mine called Meikle and, we got to know each other very well. At night we used to go out beyond the front line and make ourselves comfortable in a nice shell hole that wasn't too wet and mount his Lewis Gun, so he would be there if there was a raid during the night. As a 2nd Lieutenant, I had to visit all my men for two hours in the trenches, wherever they were, and every night I used to go out to his forward position at the end of a sap, in a shell hole, and sit with him. He was the same age as myself, possibly slightly younger, and he worked for a Glasgow railway company as well as being a bookmaker's runner. We got very close; we used to have long, long talks and he would tell me all about his life. When the war broke out he said that he'd made several attempts to enlist as a sixteen year old, but had been rejected because of his inadequate chest measurements. He finally enlisted sometime in 1915 and had gone out to France a year later just as the Somme offensive began.

Corporal John Meikle VC MM

He was a tiny little chap – we had that in common – and he stammered and you wouldn't think he could say boo to a goose. His men in the Lewis Gun team really worshipped him, even though he used to frighten them. When a coalbox dropped near and the fragments whistled through the air, Meikle would say to them 'You want to watch out, boys, there's death in those pieces'. It was his form of humour. The following year he was killed in an action for which he won the Victoria Cross.

He was such an unassuming person and I am sorry that I had to live and he had to die.

In the front line it was two hours' patrolling and then four hours on a wire bed in a shallow dugout. A dugout is a funny place; it was a place where you managed to get two or three hours' sleep before you went out to do an inspection. The dugout was lit by candles, and when you got back, in the holes in the wall there would be a little twinkle and it was the eyes of a rat. You'd look round and these were reflected in the light of the candles. You got into bed and you'd quickly pull a blanket over your head, and immediately the rats ran out over the blanket and knocked over the candles and gobbled them up in a few seconds.

The whole routine was immensely tiring, and after four hours' rest you had to be practically kicked out of the dugout to do another spell of patrol. The stress was terrible. I had a fellow officer called Aubrey Finch. He was a little older than I was, and we had an argument one time. I was a little pickled and I threw a glass of whisky in his face, which was a terrible thing to do to a fellow officer.

Stress bred fear, without doubt. You are always frightened. Mind you, most didn't show it. Men made every excuse if they were shaking or their teeth were chattering, which happened to me on more than one occasion. You just pretended it was something else, it was cold or something like that.

I remember one occasion: my teeth started to chatter because we were under a bombardment and I was in a hole in the side of a trench and the Sergeant was making me a cup of tea, making it with a candle and a billy can. In any case my teeth started chattering and I apologised to him and said 'It's so cold, isn't it?' Actually I knew perfectly well that my teeth were chattering because I didn't like the shells dropping closer and closer, and he said 'Yes, it is cold, Sir,' and passed it off, you see. And then it stopped and you pulled yourself together, but I don't mind admitting I was never the stuff that heroes were made of.

To ease the pressure we smoked; almost every man seemed to smoke. Cigarettes were a great comfort and, at the right time, worked wonders. My favourite was a brand called Passing Cloud and I recall in many stressful circumstances lighting a cigarette, although out of view of the Germans.

Most of the cigarettes were terrible and were hardly worth smoking. The cheap cigarette was the Woodbine. The Players and Goldflake were quite good ones, sixpence for twenty or fivepence ha'penny for Players. Although I might smoke up to 40 or 45 cigarettes a day, I never inhaled, so I can't say that I was a great addict, but some men would take the end of a cigarette and relight it and, even though it was saturated in tar and nicotine, they'd enjoy it.

Smoking was all part of the camaraderie and of course it relieved

Norman wearing a German cap stands in front of the ruins of Fampoux. His previously young face looks drawn.

stress, no doubt about it, it's a drug that relieved stress. You wouldn't sit smoking in the dark in a trench, or you'd soon have a few whizz bangs come over. However, behind the lines, the men used to gather together, light a cigarette, and you could see the ends glowing in the dark. There's no doubt about it, cigarettes relieved strain and stress. They were highly prized.

After several days in the line we were withdrawn to the ruined village of Fampoux, where I slept the night there amongst the ruins, in a little room. For the next few days, the battalion was employed cleaning up, while some of the men took the chance to bathe in the nearby canal, of which I retain some snaps.

Editor: *The line held by the Seaforth Highlanders in front of Roeux was the final position attained during the Battle of Arras. The following day, the 17th, the battle officially ended. It had lasted 39 days in total and the British Army had suffered around 159,000 casualties, or over 4,000 a day, the worst casualty rate for any battle fought by the British Army during the war. The 51st Division had lost 6,500 officers and men.*

A few hours relaxation for the men of Norman's platoon, seen here bathing in a canal near the River Scarpe.

May 24 1917
Dear all
....we are holding a reserve line now and not having a bad time.

The worst of open warfare is there are no dug-outs when we are shelled heavily. We stuck a 17 hour shelling the other day. Of course 'the Boche are getting short of shells' see *Daily Mail*!

I got a few souvenirs including the ribbon of an Iron Cross. I enclose it in this letter.....

Au revoir
Best love
Norman xxx

Editor: *Norman's letters had, by 1917, visibly changed from those he wrote earlier in the war. The youthful exuberance and zest for all things military had waned, and as his own learning curve began to plateau, so his desire to write long, informative, letters faded. He was now a veteran at the age of just twenty, and, for much of the rest of the war, his letters became shorter and more to the point. The impression that the conflict was wearing Norman down mentally can be gleaned, even when his writing remained at times quite optimistic.*

May 28th 1917

Dear all

Many thanks for your letter of the 21st.

Did you receive a lot of picture postcards (Boche) that I sent?

The weather is still very hot here. I am surprised that it is not in England. The Battalion is going into the front line for a few days tonight, but I am not going in this time.

The night we were relieved last week my headquarters (just an old door with two inches of soil over the trench) got a direct hit by a shell and finished 3 officers and a Sergeant Major of the regiment that relieved us [Ed. *4th Gordon Highlanders*]. Lucky for me wasn't it.

The Boche aeroplanes are very busy at present. I see in today's paper that you have had them in England.

Some of the Boche prisoners are very pessimistic while others are still confident that they will win. There are a lot of local 'scraps' in this sector but the main battle here is finished.

I had a swim in the River [Scarpe] yesterday. It was lovely.

I had my eyes tested the other day and would like you to send me out the enclosed prescript. (The result of shell explosion on December 8th 1916)

I also enclose the type of rimless I want.

3/6/17

Dear Bolton

Many thanks for your letter of the 30th.

Tomorrow we are going on a long 'trek'. We are rather in the 'dumps' tonight. You remember old Pitcairn (another little drink) that pal of mine? Well last night his brother who is in the Mechanical Transport came over to see him. They have not met for 18 months.

We had a fine time and arranged a football match for today Seaforths v Mech. Transport.

We got word tonight that Pitcairn's brother [Ed. *2nd Lieutenant Hugh Francis Pitcairn*] was killed going back to his transport column. He had an accident on his motorbike. A bit of a tragedy isn't it?

...Best love to all

Yours, Norman

Editor: *On the day of the great assault on the Messines Ridge, 7th June, the Battalion moved to the village of La Panne, where the men were billeted for a fortnight. In the countryside around La Panne the Seaforths underwent extensive training while, off-duty, men of Norman's company made friends with the local inhabitants. Norman took many pictures of this period out of the line.*

June 10th 1917

Dear all

...Oh the wounds you ask about were mere scratches as I said before, and were better long ago.

We are now many miles from the place I last wrote from, and not very far from 'Blighty'. I much prefer this part of France to the Somme, and Arras districts. There is a 'push' on at present I believe. I wish I could see a paper to know all about it.

We are 'resting' at present. Very hard work it is too.

Thanks for the cigarettes from Robinsons. I've been expecting them for a month at least. I hadn't any at all when I went into action about 3 or 4 weeks ago.

About time the war was over isn't it.

Yours with love, Norman xxx

June 17th 1917

Dear all

...I wish this war was over. It is absolute murder now. There is too much machinery about it. I hope it finishes about next spring then I can have a nice six months holiday during the fine weather. I am afraid this is a dream though as we will not be demobilised for at least 12 months I should think.

Why did I join the infantry? And an assaulting Division at that. I think the Royal Garrison Artillery would have suited my 'gentle disposition' better.

You can see I am in a fed up mood today. Probably the heat is the cause, the weather is very hot.

Well tea is ready so au Revoir

Best love to all

Norman

PS Letters from England are not censored.

June 23/1917

Dear all

Many thanks for the nice parcel you sent.

I nearly finished it in one night. A wee French kiddie about 5 years of age assisted me. You will see her photo soon.

When we left our last billet (yesterday) the people belonging to the farm shed about a bucketful of tears.

They were very good to us giving us honey, milk etc for nothing.

For a week or so I was sleeping in white sheets.

My French is improving greatly.

...With best love, Norman xx

Norman

I remember that farm at Poperinge behind Ypres and it was a delightful little place to be while we were training for 3rd Ypres. It was lovely sunny weather and, when we got time, we used to ride on the farm horses. You only had to be two or three miles behind the lines and you were back home.

There were no young men there at the farm, but it was full of their children. I have snapshots of the little girl, I mentioned her in my letter: her name was Denise and she was riding on my shoulders, and I should think she was about seven years of age. I also have pictures of my bearer, Simpson. He was aged just 18, but had been at the front fully a year and a half, having enlisted well under age. He had been a farm boy and for recreation used to hoe the vegetables on the farm, just because he wanted to do it: it was a relief for him. And I watched him on many occasions hoeing these vegetables and wondered what he was thinking about. When he returned, the farmer gave him a bottle or two of cider or wine; he certainly deserved it.

Not all relations between British troops and local people were entirely happy. I did have an occasion when, on a French farm, they locked up the water pump in the farmyard to stop us from drinking it, and this caused a little ill feeling at the time. But life in an infantry battalion was generally very circumscribed and we hardly heard French spoken at times, never mind mixing with them, except when we were right out on rest, as we were that June.

Denise. Children were a great delight to officers and men battle-worn from months serving near the line.

This period of rest was marred by one incident in which I was required to attend a court martial. Discipline was vital to the effectiveness of any army and a system of punishments were meted out to those who misbehaved. As officers we learnt all about military law and Field Punishment during training, and of course its applications. Later, in France, I saw Field Punishment No1 in operation, when the victim or culprit was spread-eagled on the wheel of an artillery wagon and strapped by the ankles and the wrists. He was in full sun and he remained tied there for the requisite

A collection of pictures taken by Norman when the Battalion was out at rest at a farm near Poperinge.

number of hours he had been sentenced to. More serious still were the punishments handed out at the court martial which could include the ultimate sanction of death.

There was to be a court martial of two men: one was a of a man who had a family of about six children and the other was an officer in a Highland Regiment. My job was as an 'officer's friend' – an officer had a personal guard. I was in charge of an officer during the day: I had to look after him for twenty-four hours and we got to know each other quite well and had a chat. He told me quite a few things about himself. He had taken too much rum when he had gone over the top and he was incapable of carrying out his duty properly. He was a charming man and I felt very sorry for him and I knew the least punishment he could get would be to be reduced to the ranks and sent back to the regiment as a private. But the next day he shot himself, and of course they wanted to know where he got the revolver from. Well he didn't get it from me and I was able to prove that, but I was almost court martialled because I was the last one with him. Obviously some brother officer had managed to slip him a revolver and got it back again after he had shot himself.

I remember the officers of the court martial, all spick and span; they were mounted and had their horses tied up there, and they all had these fly whisks you get amongst cavalry officers – they seemed in another world. They were discussing amongst themselves about the court martial, and I remember one private, as I was told at the time, was sentenced to be executed, and he was duly shot. He was a man about 35 or more with a family of about six or seven children. I have no recollection of seeing him; but I was told by one of the officers at the court martial that he had been sentenced to death. [Ed. *no soldier executed during this period seems to fit the man described and it would seem likely that, in this particular example the death sentence was commuted – as happened in 90 per cent of cases.*] There were two or three other less serious cases too. There was one of a lesser offence, and this concerned an officer who was reduced to the ranks. The battalion was paraded and the officer stood out in the middle and his badges of rank were cut off, and he was marched away and rejoined his regiment. I heard afterwards from someone who knew him that he made a very good second start and rose to the rank of Sergeant Major.

Editor: *The 51st Division, including the 4th Seaforth Highlanders, was, as the Battalion's War History noted, 'a body of shock troops – that is, troops used almost exclusively for attack. While there were obvious disadvantages in belonging to shock troops, there was the great advantage that they did not have the monotony of holding the trenches when there was nothing of interest going on, but went back for rest and training.' Those early summer months of June and July were undoubtedly the most pleasant spent by Norman in France, and he took time to take many pictures of the Battalion as it prepared for the next offensive. The War History noted games of cricket, bathing and sports in the afternoons, after morning training, while concerts and torchlight tattoos were held in the evenings.*

Norman

It was a very agreeable interlude. I still remember the scent of the broad beans and it still brings back the memory of that period whenever I smell them growing today, a lovely sweet smell. I have pictures of Pitcairn and Captain Harris, the pipe band and boxing matches between the troops, as well as pictures of the men advancing in open order and practising their musketry. Apart from training, the battalion went on several route marches. In hot weather these route marches were exhausting and we had a rest of ten minutes in the hour when, on a signal, all the men flopped down without removing their packs and just lay there until the order came to get on their feet again. And the band would strike up, the bagpipes, and off we went for another part of the route march, and very glad we were too to see the billet again.

New drafts were sent out to join the Battalion, including an officer friend of mine from Ripon, George Robson. After the mauling the Battalion had had at Arras, we were now once again more or less up to strength, fit and ready for the next offensive. And that is how it was. If you survived one assault, you went back; you trained again for another show, when once again you had to accept that your chances of living could be cut to minutes and seconds. Still, our spirits were high and, in a letter I sent home at the time, I firmly believed that the war would soon be over: 'I think we will have them out of Belgium by the end of August, at any rate we will do our best,' I wrote optimistically.

Of the proposed plan of attack itself, timed, we were told, for 31st July, my chief recollection is of a large model constructed of the front line, second and third lines at Ypres. A wooden tower had been built, like a

The 4th Seaforths on the march, encouraged by their pipers.

At work and play. The 4th Seaforths training for the forthcoming attack at Ypres while, below, the company turn out to watch a boxing match.

clay pigeon shooting tower, and officers and NCOs went to the top of this tower and looked down on a very large-scale replica of the ground over which the attack was to be made. Everything was shown, including hills, trees and field boundaries, as well as the various German pillboxes. While we were there, we were invited to walk on and around the model to familiarise ourselves with the layout, from the jumping-off trenches right back as far as a river known as the Steenbeek, some two thousand yards or more from our front line.

Editor: *Just before the Battalion moved back into the line, into the line the training intensified. 'We are very busy at present,' Norman wrote 4 July. Noting that he was not due for leave for another six months, he candidly hoped 'to get another "Blighty" before the next offensive due at the end of the month'. As with all such attacks, Norman recorded that half of the officers would be left behind, to form the backbone of the battalion in the event of heavy casualties amongst those officers taking part: 'I hadn't the luck to be left out of the show,' he*

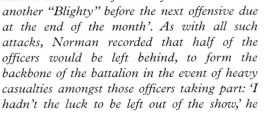

Below, a model of a battlefield built to help soldiers familiarise themselves with the terrain over which they would attack. A platform gives the opportunity for a better view.

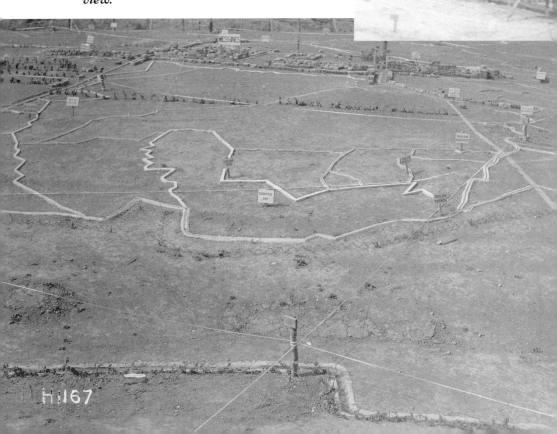

German dead strewn around the battlefield.

remarked, adding, 'the next will be my third big show'.

In the event Norman's speculative wish for a 'Blighty' was about to materialise and he would play no part in what turned into a four month struggle for the ridges to the east of Ypres.

After their quiet spell in June, in which the whole of 154 Brigade suffered not a single casualty, the men prepared themselves to return to the line. On 9 July, the 4th Seaforth Highlanders marched to St Omer, where they entrained for Poperinge, arriving around 2pm, when they marched into camp. The following day, B and C Companies were detailed to move into the support trenches near the village of Pilckem. The Battalion diary records that 10 July was a 'Dull day. 2 Lt WN Collins was slightly wounded by shrapnel. Battalion relieved the 6th Gordons in the line to the left of Ypres'.

Norman's injury was exceptionally unlucky and was caused by the occasional shellfire which accompanied B and C Company's progress into the line. He was the only officer casualty that day, although six other ranks were also wounded, possibly in the same explosion. No other casualty was recorded in the entire Brigade on the 10th; indeed, Norman was the only officer casualty that the 4th Seaforth Highlanders suffered until the final day of the month.

As Norman mentioned in his letter, had he not been wounded, he would have taken part in the new offensive, generally known as the Third Battle of Ypres. On that day, the 51st Division alone achieved all its objectives, reaching the River Steenbeek. The 4th Battalion was held in reserve to be called forward at any moment. In the event they were largely onlookers as other battalions in the Division swept forward, although the 4th Seaforths still suffered 100 casualties during the day's fighting.

Telegram
July 15th
Regret to inform you 2/Lt W N Collins 4 Seaforth admitted Duchess Westminsters Hospital 12 July Gun shot wound left leg high.

Norman

I have rather less memory of the second explosion that got me. We had begun to move up and, by a stroke of luck, a shell selected me, and this time it buried me. I know this only because I later discovered that my finger nails had all been ripped off as I sought to scratch my way out. In the end others dug me out, apparently. I can only imagine that I must have lost consciousness; I was certainly confused for sometime afterwards.

I can't remember the first part of my journey down the line, but I finally got down to a field dressing station made of corrugated iron where there were a number of casualties, including chaps with head wounds, their brains practically hanging out. At first the medics didn't know what was wrong with me until they discovered a wound in the groin, a wound in the knee, a broken scapula, as well as various other odds and ends. I must have been fairly well damaged, but most of it was internal. Patched up, I was sent down by train to the base and the Duchess of Westminster's Hospital at Paris Plage. The hospital had been set up in the Casino, a luxurious place, and I was very happy to be there, I must admit.

At the hospital I found a very nice bunch of nurses and, as I had my little camera with me, I took pictures of them. The surroundings were

The casino at Paris Plage which was turned into an officers' hospital.

Nurses relax between shifts. Spot the twins.

nice to begin with and the nurses all seemed to be jolly: they always seemed to be laughing. I think you'll see from the photographs that they are putting on a very good face. Every day the men had to have a fresh dressing, and small wounds like mine meant nothing. I mean the real wounds were where people had been almost disembowelled and still survived, and the nurses had to dress them. You would hear men who were probably dying, really, and they were calling for their mothers. A shell or a gun shot was no respecter of where it was going to hit and, in many cases, well, without going into details, you can well imagine that there's a great deal of private parts removed as well, and the nurses had to dress those, if the man survived.

You would try to disguise the pain in front of the nurses, but I never saw any nurse show signs of

LOCAL CASUALTIES.

Mr. and Mrs. F. Collins, of Rowell-street, Hartlepool, have received official intimation that their son, Second-Lieut. Norman Collins, Seaforth Highlanders, has received a gun-shot wound in the leg and been admitted into hospital. Lieut. Collins has been twice previously wounded.

weakness. Had they shown any it would have been only natural, because you've got to remember that a nursing sister with her red cloak, she's a very different kettle of fish to a VAD [Ed. *Voluntary Aid Detachment*]. The VADs were volunteers and had very little training of any kind, and naturally they would react in a human way to any pain they saw or heard, sure to; but they were very brave indeed.

The VADs we met were often from well-to-do families, whereas the general nurses were often from quite humble backgrounds and had spent many years working their way up the nursing ladder. I saw a party of VADs performing a little charade – near my bed – and one of them took the part of Queen Victoria. She had a sort of mobile face and she used to sit up and put a paper crown on, and it seemed to me that she actually knew Queen Victoria; and the nurses, the VADs who gathered around her, knelt at her feet. There were no regular nurses amongst them, they were all VADs, and I would say that many were the daughters of aristocratic families, or people out of the top drawer as the saying goes, and they were obviously – I hate using the word – a different class, a different social standing to the nurses. They had lived on every comfort and for them it must have been a great change to go and have to empty bedchambers as their first job in the morning. I salute them for everything they did in that way, because it was just as valuable as the actual dressing of a wound which was done by the regular Sister.

The nurse was very professional. She came in with her cape on and her

Paris Plage in July 1917. Looking at the photographs, it is difficult to believe that there was a war on.

voice was always very firm. She tended to order the lower ranks about, the VADs, who socially were probably higher than she was. I never saw any quarrelling, and I can only say the regular nurse knew what she wanted and saw that she got it.

It was the VADs who did the entertaining: they used to have fancy dress competitions and things like that, but these displays for our well-being never included the nurse. She got on with her job, but the VAD was allowed a little time to fraternise with the patient, which may have even have been looked upon as part of her duties.

At Paris Plage you felt then that you were living again, you were back in a civilized world: in fact I found that part of the French coast very sophisticated. They had French holidaymakers there and we used to walk and sit on the sands and you would hardly realise there was a war on. We had come from something unbelievable, a different world, and the nurses' kindness helped you to get back. I think it helped me avoid any real trauma. These VADs, if you can call them counsellors, played a great part towards the resuscitation of the wounded soldier by their kindness.

After a few weeks I was taken to England and carried on board the hospital ship on a stretcher, and I remember the Sergeant who was calling out the records as I went on board saying, 'left leg amputated', and I said 'Not at all. There's nothing wrong with it.' In those days I believe wrong things were cut off in hospital, and I was very anxious to make it clear that my left leg was not amputated and had no intention of being amputated.

CHAPTER EIGHT

Rest and Recuperation

Editor: *From August until the following June, Norman was either in hospital or convalescing at a private home. Many of the nation's wealthier home owners willingly (or grudgingly) apportioned parts of their estates to the care of wounded officers and men whose immediate medical requirements had been met by the army but who simply needed more time for the body to heal itself properly. For a great many there were mental scars too, and for these men the contemplation of yet another return to France and the trenches was hard to accept, if not anathema. As Norman says, 'Most soldiers, once they got back to England, did not wish to go back. Some pretended to be still ill, 'swinging the lead', we called it. I know it went on, although no one would tell you that they were doing it. I may have done it myself unconsciously. However, we were kept under very close scrutiny by our brother officers, and I cannot think that I found any method to convince the doctors, in my case, that I deserved to be kept any longer than was necessary. This said, a long time after everything had healed up, I was sent convalescent. The doctors probably felt sorry for me and thought I was only a young boy, so they did not push me.' It was often the care and attention of nurses and particularly VADs that acted as the best therapy for long-term patients, especially as news continued to filter through that friends, who had remained at the front, had become casualties. For soldiers in hospital, as well as families at home, it was nigh impossible to resist reading down the casualty lists that filled the papers, when 2,000 men a day were killed or wounded at the front on a daily basis; and Norman was no exception.*

Ward C1, Hyde Park Hospital
Plymouth
Aug 3rd 1917
Dear all

You will have received my telegram I expect. I arrived here at 5am after crossing on the same boat as I did last time. Curious wasn't it? I was a stretcher case.

The hospitals are crowded with wounded. 800 officers landed at Dover yesterday alone. The Seaforths had heavy casualties. I know all the killed and wounded of the 6th Batt, but have not heard about the 4th yet. I was going over with them but missed it as I was hit.

We were practising the show since June. For two months before the show we had a bad time as Fritz was putting over 10 shells to our one.

We did not want to give our own positions away. In one day at Arras we had 200 casualties from shellfire alone.

Our aeroplanes were never to be seen either as we were saving them for the big show.

All the first objectives have been gained. The Guards were next to the 51st Division.

All my kit has come across with me this time.

Will write later.

Best love, Norman.

August 25th 17

Dear Bolton

...I had a Medical Board yesterday [*to assess Norman's wounds*] and am now awaiting a transfer into a convalescent hospital where I will stay for about a month. I will not be fit for active service for some time yet. The trench fever and wound etc have taken it out of me a bit.

Will you send me the film of the VADs and nurses of the Duchess of Westminster's hospital? I promised to send them out so that they could get some printed.

When I am fit for light duty I will get 3 weeks' leave.

There isn't much news.

The weather is rotten.

Much love to all. YLB, Norman

Ward C3

Dear mother

...It is nearly 2 months since I came into hospital.

I am still at Plymouth but expect to go to a convalescent hospital in Cornwall any day. It has been raining for about a week.

I am getting quite an old soldier now and am not coming out of hospital until I am kicked out. It is the best place when there is a war on.

On July the 1st [1916] we had 50,000 casualties. I expect the Bosche had twice that. The only peace we want is unconditional surrender. We'll do it if it takes 20 years. I can't understand civilians who are not having a bad time at all, wanting to stop the war.

I don't expect to go out again this year. When I come out of the convalescent hospital I get 3 weeks leave and then 2 months light duty at Ripon.

Best love to all, Norman xxxx

Editor: *A couple of weeks later Norman was sent to a Devonshire village called Buckfastleigh and to a private house called Bigadon. The owner had offered her home for the care of officers and had then become the matron herself, presiding*

The officers' Convalescent Hospital at Bigadon in Devon.

over the home's 'efficient' running. Unwilling to submit himself to rules and regulations he deemed superfluous, Norman inevitably brought himself into conflict with the kindly matriarch who, in the end, lost patience with the young subaltern.

Ward 3, 'Bigadon'
Officers' Auxiliary Hospital
Buckfastleigh, Devon
12/9/17
Dear all
I arrived here today. I just got about 2 hours notice to move. It is a private house and holds about 50 patients. We are 2 miles from a small village and have to be in at 6pm at night. Here I hope to develop into a country joskin. I believe there is some fishing here.
Will let you know when I know all about it.
....fondest love, Norman xxxx

Oct 1917
Dear Bolton and all
...You would see the report of Robson's death. Do you know his photo? It is the big man in khaki trousers taken with some snow in the background.

Three other officers were killed and four wounded on the same day. My servant [Simpson] also went west last week. He was just 19 and had been out two years, being wounded at Beaumont Hamel. If you ever want to get news of the 4th Seaforths get the 'Ross-shire Journal'; it gives reports of the Ripon Battalion as well.

I haven't been out today. Am getting fed up with hospital. As soon as I am fit I am applying for the Indian Army. I've had enough of France.

There isn't much news. I expect to get a Board in a week or so and will probably have another month in hospital.

Bye Bye

Yours Norman

PS Robson enlisted the same week as I.

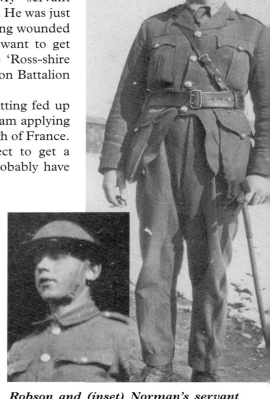

October 29th 1917

Dear old thing!

I have been laid up off and on with pains and a cold.

I often go out with the ferrets. Altogether I have got about 40 rabbits and three pheasants. Once I went to Plymouth and stayed there two days on 'French leave' [Ed. *leave without permission*]. No one spotted it.

Robson and (inset) Norman's servant Simpson. Simpson was killed after serving at the front for two years.

Last night a raiding party left our trenches (via Billiard room window) at 11pm and entered on enemy orchard returning with numerous prisoners in the shape of best 'Devonshires'.

I am quite all right, just going to have a game of billiards. 32 in my last break. I often make twenty.

Cheerio, Norman.

Sunday 11 November 1917

Dear Bolton and all

Most of my time is spent shooting. I got 28 rabbits and two brace of pheasants in three days. Eleven bunnies in eleven consecutive shots! Every day I have tea at a farm. We have about half-a-pound of cream each! Apples are as common as blackberries here.

I don't see why farmers at home object to having rabbits shot off. As a rule they are only too glad to get anyone to do it.

I am very fed up with this hospital. I've been threatened six times by the matron to be sent to Plymouth for 'bad conduct'.

Sh!

YLB Norman

Norman

We were well on the road to recovery and the nurses there used to come and show the officers their photograph albums and fraternise, perhaps asking if we wanted a book read to us. There was some romance there but that was kept as far as possible from the eyes of the matron. She was a bit of a tartar and she frowned on that sort of thing, although it went on just the same.

She didn't have many staff. The nurses used to know enough to get out for an evening, nipping out and finding their way into the bushes. There was lots of romance, I mean lots of young officers with nothing to live for; they didn't know if they were going to be back in France within weeks and be dead the next month.

I used to organise dinner parties in a nearby farmer's house where the farmer's wife would put on a wonderful dinner, often a big joint of pork. We always used to drink far too much home-grown cider and then we used to go back in the pony trap, singing quite heartily, which brought me into disfavour with the matron. I knew she would be listening and saying, 'Is that that Collins again?' And, if we knew she was within earshot, we would be singing at the top of our voices some rude verses about her. If she had had any sense of humour – she may have had for all I knew – she would have appreciated them because they were never

The pony and trap used to ferry officers and nurses to the nearby farm for dinner.

vicious, just leg pulling.

I was fond of one of the nurses in particular and occasionally, in the evening, I made a point of taking her out to the farmhouse for dinner, with nobody's knowledge except the farmer's wife. We used to have a nice bit of roast lamb and a glass of cider. It didn't lead to any permanent romance because at that age you haven't got a career and you can't think of marriage. Things were kept quiet, I mean, people didn't walk about in broad daylight, but equally I don't think we cared about any repercussions. We didn't worry about trivial things. Inevitably, I suppose, I was sent away to Devonport, a very austere hospital altogether. I quickly realised my error and, after an interview with the senior medical officer, I was sent to Plymouth, much to my relief.

WNC Block A
Royal Military Hospital
Devonport
21.11.17
Dear all
I left Buckfastleigh on Monday morning. I couldn't get on very well with the matron and so I was sent here 'for further treatment'.

I will soon have completed five months in hospital. In about a month's time I ought to be fit enough for light duty. I discovered when I was leaving the hospital on Monday that a gun [Ed. *sent earlier by Bolton*] had arrived about six weeks ago but the Matron had hidden it! She is very childish in that way. I have got it here.

In this hospital we are only allowed out from 2pm to 6pm. There isn't even a billiard table or a gramophone in the place.

Bye Bye,
best love Norman

Fraternisation.

The billiard room at Bigadon hospital.

Durnford Mill Hospital
Stonehouse
Plymouth
Dear Bolton, Mum and Dad
...You will see I am in another hospital. The fifth since I was wounded! It is a great improvement on the last one. I have a little room with only two beds in. There is a billiard table here. I am quite A1 and will probably be out of the clutches of the RAMC by February or earlier.

Dec 18 1917
Dear Mum and Dad
Three days leave is being granted for Xmas but it isn't worth coming home for just a day. Besides it would cost me about £5 and I am broke.

I am awfully sorry to hear of Tom Weatherhead's death [Ed. *a friend from Hartlepool*]. He couldn't have been long in the army. What regiment was he in?

...You needn't send a cake. You will need all the food you can get I suppose. If you can raise a subscription for about 10/- it would be much more to the point as I spent £10 on a gramophone and records and in consequence am in a state of extreme poverty until the 1st of Jan. It is a rotten war when one is broke. I will have to mortgage my estates or sell the family jewels.

I am in perfect health and went about thirty miles into the country yesterday to shoot rabbits. I didn't miss a shot (killed six in an hour) and all were running.

I could let you have half a dozen Seaforth buttons from my old tunic. I will be sending some stuff home soon when I have the energy to sort my valise. I have a tin hat here that's no use. You could wear it for church or during air-raids!

YLS Norman

Jan [1918]
Dear Mother and all.

...my sergeant at the front got a commission and on arriving in England fell out of a window and broke his neck! He has been out for three and a half years and thro' every show from Neuve Chapelle without a scratch!

Bye Bye, Norman

Thursday
Dear B

...I tried to get weekend leave this week (last week was an unofficial one) but was refused. It is very difficult to get leave now. My total leave in a year is 48 hours and the one I took last week. ...I'm fed up with doing parades. It is getting too strict. I wish I was farther north or back in dear old Devon, with 'little Willie' the ferret and the gun ...I could get a few days leave in H'pool if anyone was ill and I was wired for. That would be the only way.

Cheerio, Norman

Norman with his faithful ferret 'Little Willie'.

180

Officers relaxing at Bigadon, playing tennis, rugby, quoits and tug-of-war.

Command Depot Eastbourne (Grand Hotel)
Tuesday, February 1918
Dear Mum and Dad
...This is quite a decent place except that the food is awful.

I have dinner every night at this Hotel. It is a magnificent place; about six times the size of the West H'pool Grand and is one of the largest in England. To see the dining room at night one would hardly think there was a war on. It is crowded with people in evening dress like pre-war times. I expect to be there three months. I haven't had my Feb 1st board yet and do not expect it this month.

We have plenty of freedom here and we are allowed out as late as we like although officially it is 11pm. I am quite well, we do very little work here. A short walk at a snail's pace and a few games of quoits. It is rather funny to parade for games and get the order 'fall out the quoits party' or the 'rounders party'!

Every fortnight we are examined by the M.O. and placed in a higher category if we are better. The work gradually gets harder. There are six categories. I am in No4. A fortnight today I will probably be in No3. When we have had about a fortnight or month in No1 we are discharged G[eneral]S[ervice] or Home Service.

Yours with dearest love, Norman.

February 1918
Officer Command Depot Eastbourne
Dear B
I arrived in Eastbourne about 9am last Monday. Up to the present (Wed) I have appeared on parade to answer my name and then 'sloped'. The Midland Hotel and St Pancras Station were hit by bombs on the night of Sunday-Monday about midnight. I arrived at St Pancras 5 hours afterwards.

This afternoon I am to be examined by the MO and if he thinks I am getting better will be moved up one into Group 3. We usually have a fortnight in each group. At present I am in No4. If I get home service for a few months at my next board, it wouldn't be a bad idea to apply for a job with the Ministry of Munitions. I could do with about six months in England. Since I have been commissioned I have spent all my time in France or in hospital.

Yours to a cinder, Norman.

Norman

I was convalescent in Eastbourne and on my 21st birthday [*16 April*] I went out for a lonely meal at the Grand Hotel. The head waiter, who had put a little patriotic flag on my table as a celebration, subsequently went and told a distinguished soldier who was also having a meal that it was my 21st birthday. The officer in question came over and briefly sat with me, and his name was General Robertson, the Quarter Master General who himself had enlisted as a private and reached the rank of Field Marshal, the only man ever to do so. Sir William was a great character and I was proud to meet him.

In the convalescent home in Eastbourne, I again met Lieutenant Pollock, the Cameron Highlander who had won the Victoria Cross. He had been wounded and now only had one eye. Occasionally we used to go down to the Grand Hotel and listen in the Palm Court there to the orchestra while on another occasion I remember going up to London with him. I remember this occasion distinctly for one incident. We were walking past Horse Guards' Parade and got quite a shock when the sentry called out 'Guard turn out'; the whole guard turned out and presented arms for Pollock because he had the VC.

[*late April*] Eastbourne
Dear Bolton

Many thanks for the cigs. How are you off for 'gaspers' up North? It is almost impossible for civilians to get them here but we can get plenty in the army canteens. If you are short let me know. The weather is awfully cold today.

The adjutant of the 4th at Ripon was killed about a fortnight ago, CM Cameron. I'm afraid old Henderson of the Argyll & Sutherland

The Grand Hotel at Eastbourne where Norman met General, later Field Marshal Robertson (1860-1933), Chief of the Imperial General Staff (inset).

The raid on the port of Zebrugge with British ships sunk in the harbour mouth.

Highlanders is nah-pooh. Pitcairn and one other were the only officers left in the battalion as I knew it last April, out of 40.

I expect we will lose Ypres (temporary).

Cheerio, Norman

PS The army is awfully ratty about the song made over the raid by the navy. One paper was talking about a special medal similar to Mons. One chap got a knighthood through it! Every battalion in the army does more in every show.

Editor: *On the night of 22/23 April the Navy launched a raid on the ports of Zeebrugge and Ostend in an attempt to block the harbour exits and thereby halt further U Boat attacks that were crippling British shipping. During the raid, old British ships filled with concrete were scuttled at the mouth of each port.*

However, the ships were sunk in the wrong place leaving the hulks to cause only minor disruption to harbour traffic. The raids were nevertheless hailed as a victory in the British Press and Commander Keyes who had planned the raid was indeed ennobled. The British suffered 500 casualties.

BACK WITH THE REGIMENT IN SCOTLAND

Editor: *Norman was finally discharged from hospital on 6th June 1918, almost eleven months after being wounded. On leaving, he was sent straight back to the 4th Reserve Training Battalion of the Seaforth Highlanders which, after May 1918, had relocated from Ripon to Glencorse near Edinburgh. The Training Battalion continued to prepare large numbers of new recruits for the front as well providing short courses of instruction for wounded or invalided men sent home from overseas.*

4th (R) Seaforth Highlanders
Glencorse Camp, Milton Bridge
Sunday June 9th
Dear all
I arrived here about 9.30 last night. My luggage is still at the station about two miles away. The only conveyance was by bus.

I know very few of the officers here. I have been detailed to attend a course of instruction on Gas or Stokes guns or something. The course is at Edinburgh and I get 8/- a day extra while I am there which will only be for a few days.

The Seaforths have sent over 100 officers away to France in a month. Thank goodness I'm for service in the East. The only recruits we are getting are the boys of 18 years of age.

Best love,
Norman

Editor: *It is not clear when, but by the time Norman arrived at Glencorse he had already applied to join the Indian Army. 'I had seen a piece in a paper stating that two regular commissions in the Indian Army were being offered and I thought that instead of going back to France, I would like a change and I applied.' After two tours of duty in France, and over a year in various hospitals, Norman was keen to avoid another spell on the Western Front. In contrast to his apparent optimism in the previous note home that he was for 'service in the east', Norman was in fact unsure that officer casualties in France would not necessitate his own return to the fighting. In a note written home, his concern is clear, 'If I don't get my papers in I can be sent to France any day, so I wish they would hurry up', he wrote. While he waited for an interview board, Norman was sent to several refresher classes.*

Marine Hotel
Troon
Wednesday
12.6.18
Dear all

I am getting quite used to work again...This is a fine course. It is partly lectures and partly practical work. We have been firing nearly all day. Each gun has a crew of five. No1 gives the orders. No2 sights and fires the gun. No3 helps to fix it up and 4 and 5 fix up the shells for firing.

I am No2. The shells are quite big affairs over a foot long and weigh about 12 lbs. The range is 800 yards. The fire is so rapid that one gun can get eight shells in the air at once, before the first hits the ground.

I drop the shells in the muzzle and they slide down the gun and hit a striker at the bottom which explodes the propelling cartridge at the bottom of the shell, which then flies out. About six shells will blow a house to bits.

The only thing to be careful about is to get your hands away from the muzzle as soon as you drop the shell in, otherwise they will go with the shell.

I have heard unofficially that Henderson was a prisoner in Germany. He will probably write if that is so. Norman

A Stokes mortar in action.

Norman

I went through any number of courses to get me ready for a possible trip back to France. I went to Penicuik and had a course there on the .45 revolver. I had carried a .45 when I had gone abroad in 1916 but it was so heavy it was impossible to hit a barn door at 10 yards. At Penicuik we were taught how to use it properly. For the first five or six days, the instructor did not allow us to do anything more than point the revolver with a straight wrist at the target, using both hands. We were kept hard at it with one revolver unloaded, doing nothing else but lifting it hundreds of times and keeping the forefinger straight. And then we did the same thing with two .45s until our forearms were like rods of iron.

The instructor then showed us what could be done. He could take a penny and he could hit this with his .45 revolver every time; he was a remarkable man. We then were allowed to fire live ammunition, which we did day after day until the end of the course. In the final test, we had to fit a gas mask on, jump into a trench with two revolvers, and cardboard figures appeared and we had to fire at both. The trick for this, we were told, was to look at the two figures with peripheral vision, to look straight ahead and bisect the distance between the two, look at that, raise the revolvers with rigid forearms and fire, and in many cases we managed to hit both at the same time.

As a finale, the instructor demonstrated another trick that seems almost impossible. He took a number of empty cartridge cases and put them in holes in a plank of wood, so that they had support, and whilst he couldn't fit the bullet back into the case on every occasion, I saw him do it on more than one occasion, and in any case he buckled the case up every time. To make a fit of the bullet back into the case seems impossible but it actually happened, and I saw it happen.

Long afterwards, I met this instructor in West Hartlepool, where he was an opera singer taking the part of *Faust*, and he gave me a few tickets to watch him; it takes all sorts to make a world.

Having completed this course, which lasted about a fortnight, I suppose, not knowing what to do with me, the regiment sent me off to Troon again, on the west coast of Scotland where I was billeted at the Troon Hotel. We practised near the golf course there, courses that consisted of the bomb and the bayonet. We were taught how to handle Mills bombs by an instructor who seemed to have no fear whatever of them. First of all, he showed us the fuse that could be cut in various lengths, the normal length being one which lasted five seconds. Another fuse was instantaneous, which was a red fuse. And we were taught how to throw these bombs at given targets from the trench. We were always in the trench when we threw them, but there was also a wall to one side which we could duck behind if anything went wrong. He demonstrated how safe they were by throwing a Mills bomb, after withdrawing the pin, to an assistant instructor who caught it and threw it. This said, if the assistant missed it, he had to be very quick to pick it up and throw it over the top of the trench. It wasn't a trick that I would have liked to have done myself, but we certainly learnt to be familiar with them and we learned to handle them with great respect, because a Mills bomb can cause a lot of damage.

We had a musketry course there, when we fired over various ranges up to 800 yards, and I enjoyed this. We were taken out on night operations too, after they had buried explosive flashes in the earth during the day. We would perform various operations, patrolling at night, and occasionally a flash would go off quite close, and this of course was to simulate shellfire, but, to those who had seen something of the real thing, they didn't seem to be performing much service except for beginners who had never heard an explosion before.

We were taught gas mask drill, how to smell gas faintly; phosgene was the chief one. I had not come into first hand contact with gas at the front, although when I was in hospital, wounded, mustard gas casualties had come in and they were a terrible sight. They were walking along with their hands on the shoulders of the ones in front, and they were obviously in great pain. I had worn a gas mask when alerted to the threat of gas, but the closest I had actually been to a gas shell drop was perhaps a hundred yards or more away from me when I was at Arras. Then, I had seen some Portuguese troops, they were quite innocent, for they saw this shell drop and realised it wasn't going to go off because only a little puff of smoke had come from it. There were only half a dozen of them and they approached the shell out of curiosity. They were taken away as casualties.

Officers Concentration Camp
Dreghorn
Edinburgh
Dear Bolton and all
...I am at present on a Lewis Gun Course lasting three weeks.

Altogether since I reported for duty I have had a Trench Mortar Course, two Gas Courses, Revolver and now a Lewis Gun Course.

I haven't taken any photos since I left home as I cannot get film.

My Indian papers are at present before the Brigadier Gen. The CO recommended me. I shouldn't think I will leave before October.

...Of all the officers who were out with me last year there is only one left in France. I spoke to an Argyle who was with Henderson at the time of the German attack in March. He did very well in the first three days of the attack. On 23 March the Division was retiring according to orders and he missed Henderson and on looking round saw him lying down in

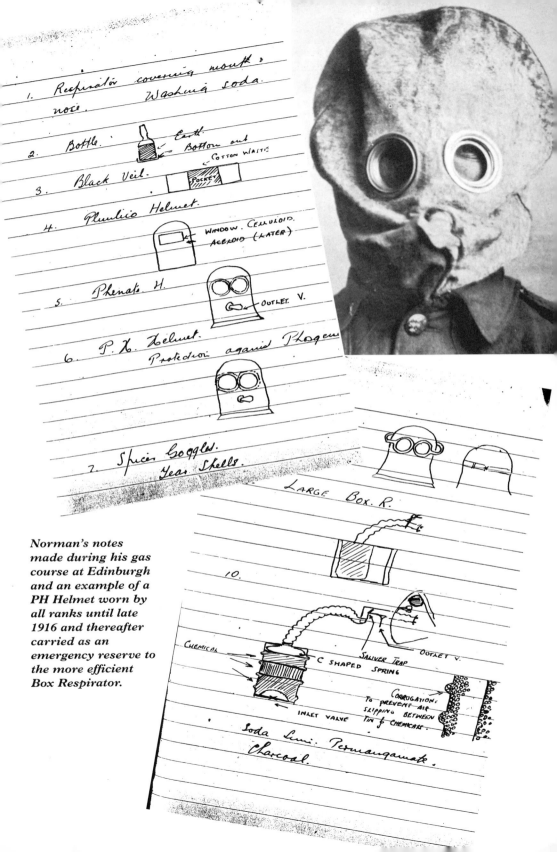

1. Respirator covering mouth, nose. Washing soda.

2. Bottle. Cork. Bottom out

3. Black Veil. Cotton Waste. Pocket

4. Plumbic Helmet. Window. Celluloid. Aceloid (later)

5. Phenate. H. Outlet. V.

6. P. H. Helmet. Protection against Phosgene

7. Spier Goggles. Tear Shells.

LARGE BOX. R.

10.

Chemical
Saliver Trap
Outlet V.
C Shaped Spring
Corrugations to prevent air slipping between Tin & Chemicals.
Inlet valve

Soda Lime. Permanganate. Charcoal.

Norman's notes made during his gas course at Edinburgh and an example of a PH Helmet worn by all ranks until late 1916 and thereafter carried as an emergency reserve to the more efficient Box Respirator.

the middle of a field with the Boche only a few yards away. He thinks he was dead or badly wounded. His relatives and fiancée have heard nothing. Exit a damned fine boy.

Cheerio, Norman.

Sunday (August 4th 1918)

Dear Bolton

....Last week I was before the GOC about India. He signed my transfer papers and sent them to the War Office. I expect to get word to report at the India Office for medical exam within the next few weeks.

The Highland Division has been mentioned in the papers lately. It marched 50 miles in two days and then attacked the same day advancing near Reims. (If I hadn't been going to India I would be in France).

Best love, Norman

Editor: *Norman was invited to London to go before a Selection Board where 'one general and a couple of other senior officers questioned me very closely as to my background and my general ability as an officer, liking for sport and so on', recalled Norman. 'Then, shortly afterwards, I received a notice saying that I had been accepted.' After 4 August there are few letters of any interest, other than general comments about the advances the allies were now making on the Western Front. The war was drawing to a close, although even then, Norman was to lose yet another friend, 27 year old Lieutenant Philip Ballantyne, who was killed in the last attack the Battalion was to make in the war, Monday 28 October 1918. Ballantyne had gone overseas with Norman in April 1917 and was probably the 'last' officer in France to whom Norman alluded to in his letter, see page 188. Two weeks later, the Armistice was signed. During the war both battalions in which Norman had served, the 4th and the 6th Seaforth Highlanders, had each lost well over 1,000 officers and men killed in action.*

CHAPTER NINE

The Armistice and the Aftermath

On the day of the Armistice I was on leave and staying with an aunt and uncle of mine in Sheffield. I was up a bit late that morning and was shaving when the sirens and hooters sounded across the city. Incredibly the war was over, but my one thought was 'It's too late – all my friends are gone – it's too late. It's no good having an Armistice now.'

I had a vision, and I was standing in a trench. I could not put my head up because I was under fire, but above me, at eye level, walking past were hundreds and hundreds of boots and puttees. I thought of all those I had known; it was like a panorama of passing people, people from the cadet battalion, through the various training courses and out in France. They

Jubilant crowds celebrate the Armistice.   IWM Q80175

went on and on for hours, and I realised it was the dead all walking away and leaving me behind. I felt worried and frightened that they were leaving me by myself; that I had been left behind. They were marching away into the distance, where I would never follow. All the people I knew had gone, except me. That was a vivid dream and I dreamt it on many occasions, although I never told anyone until I was a very old man, because I felt it was a private matter between my old comrades and myself. It was a most intense feeling and it remained so. I was very sad but I got over it; I must have been very resilient. From that time onwards I can only recall two people that I ever met in my life that I served with in France, and neither was a very close associate of mine.

Whilst I was glad the war was over, I was not excited about it; I did not throw my hat up or anything like that, or feel like going out and rejoicing with champagne. I felt sad. The war should have been stopped earlier: it went on far too long. I don't think anybody won, everybody lost.

The years of war seemed to last longer than all of the rest of my life put together. I remember looking at my father and thinking he had never seen a dead man, and I'd seen scores and scores of dead men. He had never seen a shot, never seen a man die. Or if he had, it would have been in family circumstances. I really felt much older than my parents, and I think that feeling continued for the rest of my life.

Shortly after the Armistice, I received word that I had to proceed to London, get some Indian Army uniform, some khaki drill. I was told to report to the Transport Office, where I received my instructions (which I still have) to get on to a ship lying off Tilbury, called the *Themistocles*, which was a ship that was used on the New Zealand route as a liner before the war. Several hundreds of officers were on board the ship when it left in December, and it was in the Mediterranean on Christmas Day. I remember the minefields were still there; we had to zig-zag in between the mines, and we arrived at Port Said, the entrance to the Suez Canal. As we anchored there, a troop ship came out of the canal with troops lining it, all looking very sunburnt, still with pith helmets on, and they all shouted 'You are all going the wrong way', which perhaps we were.

FRANCE 1989

Editor: *Norman returned to France for the one and only time 14 April 1989, two days before his 92nd birthday. He was unconcerned about such a visit even given his great age; on the contrary, he noted in his taped diary that 'I would consider it amusing, if I were able to, if I passed out 73 years after the battle on the same spot where I should have passed on at 19 years of age. I'm sure I would be greeted by cries of 'Late on parade, Sir?'*

Top, in 1989, Norman surveys Y Ravine at Beaumont Hamel. Below, standing behind the graves of his friends Smith and Mclean.

Now and then: Norman walks next to the River Scarpe where (below) he took a picture of the collapsed railway bridge which once spanned the river.

Norman

When I went to France 73 years ago, there was nothing but brick dust blown into the soil. I am going to see the real France; the villages of which, when I was out there before, there was nothing left. Then, I could only see them from the trenches with a periscope, but now I will be able to walk about freely on the battlefield and it will be an amazing sensation. Before I only had a rat's view, a worm's view of the French countryside.'

Editor: *With his son, Norman visited many places familiar to all those tourists who visit the battlefields today, including the La Boisselle mine crater, blown under the German line on July 1st 1916, and the Welsh Division memorial at Mametz Wood. He also saw the South African memorial and museum at Delville Wood, and the Thiepval memorial to the missing of the Somme. However, most importantly, Norman visited the sites where he had stood in his youth. He walked in the trenches in Newfoundland Park, orientating himself as he walked. He located the Beaumont Hamel mine crater on the horizon by the position of Y Ravine, then he walked among the grassed-over shell holes where he had buried so many Newfoundlanders in November 1916. And he visited, too, the cemetery at Maillet Wood, where so many of his friends, including Lieutenants Smith and Mclean, still lie side by side, just as he buried them. Later, Norman visited the trenches at Vimy Ridge, the Menin Gate memorial to the missing at Ypres and the battlefield around Arras. He saw the graves of many of the friends he knew, including Otto Murray Dixon and John Meikle, buried in a cemetery at Marfaux, near Reims.*

Norman

'My son asked me to return to France. We went to see Smith and Mclean and I found them still buried side by side, and I have a photograph taken of me standing between them. The grass has grown over the trenches, which have been preserved. I saw the trench from which the Newfoundlanders had taken off on July 1st and I also covered the same ground that I had been over, with the German trenches on the other side of the field, where the sheep were grazing; overhead the larks were singing. And there was a complete metamorphosis of what I had seen at the time in November 1916. I looked over the ground where I had buried all those dead, and my memory was as clear as it was over eighty years ago. I was glad to be alive, even though I was beginning to become very inactive and suffering quite a bit of pain from the old wounds. But I wondered whether they had missed much. Their mothers must have suffered horribly, and not only that, but the million young girls in England with no one for a husband, a million 'surplus' women, many alive today aged 100 years or more. What must their memories be like? I hope they got some pleasure out of life.

For a long time, the period of the war was longer than the next fifty years – it was the intensity of it. A day there was like a year anywhere else, because the chances of living were small. I have a greater chance of living a week at the age of 92 than I did when I was 19. I don't think people appreciated what had happened. The men who died are soon forgotten by those who were not there, but they are never forgotten by those of us who still remember.

I went to have a look at Meikle's gravestone and was surprised to see an entry in the cemetery book of a lady who said she'd come to see Meikle, the father she never knew. I have a lovely picture and there I am, standing looking down; and Sergeant Meikle is young bones, of course, still young bones, and there I am, nearly a hundred, standing on top – very old brittle bones with plenty of pain in them, but who won in the end? I mean, who had the better life? Nobody knows. Meikle died. Anyway he won't know, he had no memory and eventually I will go the same way.

I've been asked on several occasions in my life if I killed anyone and I refuse to answer. I'm not going to say that I killed anyone in my life, but if anybody thinks that I managed to get through that war without killing anyone, then I would like them to explain how. Your imagination can tell you a lot from what I've said and that is sufficient. But I'm not going to be drawn into how many I killed or didn't kill. I can tell you this: I was not, and never claimed to be, a brave soldier. All I did was what I considered I had to do, and that was my duty. Why did I join up? I joined up, as you call it, along patriotic lines, and I said I joined up to defend this country. There were certain things I had to do, otherwise I'd have been useless, wouldn't I?

I am very much living in the present. I very rarely dwell in the past; in fact this is quite a unique experience and I would never have come back here unless my son had asked me to. I don't live in the past at all. I haven't forgotten

Norman at the grave of Sergeant Meikle VC, MM.

it, because one can't forget, one doesn't want to forget. I mean, those two graves I saw of Smith and Mclean, the two lieutenants in my battalion, I've never forgotten them, but I don't dwell on that sort of thing. I enjoy my present life and I hope to continue a little longer, and I hope to see you in eight years time if I may.'

'When you are 100?'

'When I am 100.'

Editor: *Within weeks of returning home from France Norman was moved to write the following poem dated 5 June 1989.*

OVER THE TOP

'Twas just three minutes to zero time,
Everyone held his breath.
For in three minutes we all would go,
To Victory – or Death.

The mine went up with a thundering roar,
Then out the barrage crashed,
And the Heavens were lit with the fires of Hell,
As the storm the trenches thrashed.

Then out we raced with muffled cheers,
Into the mouth of Hell!
While machine guns took their dreadful toll,
And many a comrade fell.

We fought like devils that misty morn,
With bayonet, bomb and gun.
And right through steel and fire we charged.
The Bosche front line was won.

The wire and snipers held us up,
For perhaps an hour or more,
But again and again with glittering steel,
We charged with a sullen roar.

Our losses were heavy – 'tis always so.
But the foe was badly shaken.
Once again the Highlanders charged,
And lo – the village was taken.

And battle was over, the victory won,
And the sinking sun shone red
On the land we'd wrested from the Hun;
On the heaps of silent dead.

We called the roll at dead of night,
Under the star shells weird glare,
But many a comrade answered not,
For he'd answered the Roll up there.

Just a few square miles of country won.
And many a soldier fell,
But they died, with a smile, for their motherland,
For they'd done their duty well.

They've left their mark (a small one, true),
On the history of our land.
Gentlemen! A silent toast,
To that gallant little band.

Editor: *After his father's death in 1998, Ian Collins returned to the Somme and the Newfoundland Park. He found that the descendants of the Newfoundlanders Norman had buried in 1916 had visited the park. There, at the memorial built to honour the 51st Division's successful assault on Beaumont Hamel, three wreaths had been laid to Norman's memory.*

The following is a list of officers and other ranks killed in the Great War and who are mentioned in this book. All were known to Norman; six of them have no known grave.

Lieutenant Philip Hugh Ballantyne, 4th Seaforth Highlanders, died Monday 28th October 1918 aged 27. Son of James and Mary Annie Ballantyne of New Hill, Huddersfield. Vis-En-Artois Memorial, Pas de Calais, Panel 10.

Captain Colin Mackenzie Cameron, Adjt 4th Seaforth Highlanders, died on Thursday 11 April 1918 aged 23. Son of Colin Mackenzie Cameron and Adelaide Scott Cameron of Balnakyle, Ross-shire. Maroc British Cemetery, Nord, France I.L.46.

2/Lt Alexander James Davidson, 4th Seaforth Highlanders, died on Sunday 8 April 1917 aged 30. Son of Alexander and Mary Davidson of Dingwall. Highland Cemetery, Roclincourt, Pas de Calais, France II.D.3.

Captain Aubrey Malcolm Cecil Finch, 4th Seaforth Highlanders, died Monday 7 July 1919 aged 22. Son of William and Rona Finch of Beckenham, Kent. Archangel Allied Cemetery, Russian Federation Sp. Mem. B40.

Pte Lawrence Grigor 2779, 6th Seaforth Highlanders, KIA 13 November 1916, son of Mr J and Mrs Grigor of Haighland, Elgin, Mailly Wood Cemetery 1 E 9.

Lieutenant James Angus Henderson, 7th Bn attd 1/8th Argyll and Sutherland Highlanders, died Monday 25 March 1918 aged 27. Son of David and Isabella Henderson of Thurso, Caithness. Pozieres Memorial, Somme, Panel 77 & 78.

Private Arthur Gordon Henry 3596, B Company 6th Seaforth Highlanders, died of wounds 15 November 1916 aged 18. Son of George and Mrs Henry of 655 Hawthorn Street, Springburn, Glasgow. Thiepval Memorial Pier and Face 15C.

Lieutenant George Munro MacBey MC, 6th Seaforth Highlanders, died Friday 22 March 1918 aged 20. Son of William Monro MacBey and Catherine MacBey of Tarbert, Lossiemouth, Morayshire. Arras Memorial, Pas de Calais, Bay 8.

Private William McKenzie, KIA Monday 13 November 1916, son of George and Mrs Mckenzie of Easterton Cottage, Westerton, Speymouth, Fochabers, Morayshire. Mailly Wood Cemetery I G 5.

2/Lt Raymond Alastair Mclean, attached 6th Battalion Seaforth Highlanders, KIA 13/11/16 aged 23. Son of William and Mary Mclean of 82 Beconsfield Villas, Brighton. Native of Ross-shire.
Vans Dunlop scholar, University of Edinburgh MA with triple honours. Divinity student. Mailly Wood Cemetery I F 30.

Sergeant John Meikle VC MM, 200854 4th Seaforth Highlanders. KIA Saturday 20 July 1918 aged 19. Marfaux British Cemetery, Marne Plot 8 Row C Grave 1 On the 20 July 1918 near Marfaux, France, Sergeant John Meikle 'showed most conspicuous bravery and initiative. No.2 Company were held up by machine-gun fire, when Sergeant Meikle, advancing for some 150 yards, alone, over open ground, rushed one of the machine-gun nests single-handed, emptying his revolver into the crews of the two guns, and putting the remainder of them out of action with a heavy stick. Then standing up, he waved the company on. When, later in the day, another hostile machine gun checked the progress of the company, Meikle found that most of his platoon had become casualties. Undismayed, he seized the rifle and bayonet of a fallen comrade and again rushed forward against the gun crew. He was killed when almost in the gun position, but his bravery enabled two other men who followed him to put the gun out of action.'

Captain George James Morrison MC, 1/6th Seaforth Highlanders, died on Thursday 11 April 1918 aged 25, son of John and Margaret Morrison, of Brodie, Forres. Lapugnoy Military Cemetery, Pas de Calais VII.C.5.

2/Lt Henry Edward Otto Murray Murray-Dixon, 1/4th Seaforth Highlanders, died Tuesday 10 April 1917 aged 31 of wounds received at Vimy Ridge. Son of James Murray and Etheldreda Murray-Dixon of Swithland Rectory, Loughborough. Aubigny Communal Cemetery Extension, Pas de Calais VI.A.7.

2/Lt Hugh Francis Pitcairn, 47th Division Supply Column Mechanical Transport Army Service Corps, killed Sunday 3rd June 1917 aged 37, son of John George and Augusta Frances Pitcairn of Lee, London. Aubigny Communal Cemetery, Pas de Calais V1.G.15.

Lt George Robson, KIA Thursday 20 September 1917 aged 35. Son of George and Hannah Robson of Wellington Terrace, South Shields. Tyne Cot Memorial, Addenda Panel.

L/Cpl Alexander Simpson 265772, KIA Wednesday 19 September 1917 aged 18, son of Alexander and Mrs Simpson of Beaufont Home Farm, Beauly, Inverness-shire. Tyne Cot Panel 132-65 and 162A.

2/Lt Robert James Smith, KIA 13.9.1916, son of John and Mary Smith of East Mains, Knockando, Morayshire, land valuer (Inland Revenue), Mailley Wood Cemetery 1F 29.

Private John Thomas Weatherhead 48457, D Coy 4th North Staffordshire Regiment, died Friday 30 November 1917, son of John and Elizabeth Ann Weatherhead of 84 Northgate, Hartlepool. Mendingham Military Cemetery, Poperinge 1.G.40.

Postscript

After the war, Norman served with the 4th Rajputs Indian Army on the North West Frontier in the Waziristan campaign of 1920/21. In May 1921, he rose to the rank of Captain, before being invalided out and returning to the UK. In 1921, he began reading Engineering at Armstrong College, Durham University, from where he later took an apprenticeship with the Austin Motor Company, Longbridge. He stayed with Austin Motors for the next 13 years, being responsible for the operation of a string of service depots. At the outbreak of war in 1939, he became Chief Technical Assistant to the Director of Mechanisation (later called the Ministry of Supply, then the Ministry of Defence). Here he oversaw the requisitioning of car workshops across the country to repair battle-damaged vehicles. (Unbeknown to Norman, this was a dangerous post. It was only in the late 1980s that he discovered, quite by chance, that his name appeared on an SS hit list – along with Winston Churchill's. Given an identification number by the Germans, Norman was due for immediate execution had the Germans successfully invaded Britain in 1940.) Norman stayed in the post, rising to Deputy Director before being released in 1944 to join F Perkins Ltd. Perkins was famous for its diesel engine manufacturing, and during Norman's tenure it was to become the largest of its kind in the world. While there, he released a young office boy, Godfrey Evans, to go for trials with Kent Cricket Club. Later, as perhaps England's most famous wicket keeper, Evans presented Norman with the gloves he used to keep wicket with during England's test tour of Australia in 1953. Until his retirement in 1961, Norman held the post of Deputy Managing Director. He devoted his long retirement to shooting and fishing, until bad eyesight forced him to give up at the age of 86. He was very keen on wildlife and helped to found the Wildfowl Trust, with Sir Peter Scott. In 1989, on his return to the battlefields, he was granted the Freedom of the City of Albert, the principal town held by the British during the Battle of the Somme. 'It was this honour,' as *The Times* obituary noted, that 'he cherished above all others'.

Norman when an officer with the 4th Rajputs. The heat of India was to prove too much for his wounds, forcing him to return to England, where he was invalided out of the army.

Norman receives a cup from the Queen Mother in the 1950s.

INDEX